UNTIL THE WHEELS FALL OFF:
THE EXTRAORDINARY LIFE OF JOE PALADINO

by

Joe Paladino

The contents of this work, including, but not limited to, the accuracy of events, people, and places depicted; opinions expressed; permission to use previously published materials included; and any advice given or actions advocated are solely the responsibility of the author, who assumes all liability for said work and indemnifies the publisher against any claims stemming from publication of the work.

All Rights Reserved
Copyright © 2022 by Joe Paladino

No part of this book may be reproduced or transmitted, downloaded, distributed, reverse engineered, or stored in or introduced into any information storage and retrieval system, in any form or by any means, including photocopying and recording, whether electronic or mechanical, now known or hereinafter invented without permission in writing from the publisher.

Dorrance Publishing Co
585 Alpha Drive
Suite 103
Pittsburgh, PA 15238
Visit our website at *www.dorrancebookstore.com*

ISBN: 978-1-6853-7318-4
eISBN: 978-1-6853-7851-6

Dedications

I dedicate this book to all my spinal cord community. I hope you see my story as one of possibilities for you. It's not about how you start, but how you finish that matters.

I also dedicate this book to my late mother, Dolores "Celia" Paladino. She was my first caregiver and it is because of her love and dedication that I am still here.

Every word is dedicated to my savior, Jesus Christ. Without Him all this would be meaningless.

FOREWORD

One night, I sat in bed with Joe as we were talking about a lot of things. We were discussing the things of God and life. I looked over at him with love in my eyes and said, "One day I want to write a book about your life."

Joe laughed and said, "Why would anyone want to read that?" I just about fell off the bed. Joe's story is a miraculous chain of events that culminated in his injury, recovery, and redemption in Christ, and in life. Joe's life is one of great success but it wasn't because he was particularly educated or talented in business. He just has an incredible ability to beat the odds and to not take no for an answer. He calls it 'Hustle.' I call it guts. And he has lots of it.

As his second wife, I had the benefit of Joe learning from his mistakes in his previous marriage. But as Joe's second wife, I also had the charge of filling big shoes and doing more to care for him in his later years. Some of that care came in daily personal care, and some of it was dealing with very real mental health issues like anxiety and depression. Many saw Joe as someone to be envied due to his wealth. He often wondered how many would be willing to trade their mobility for a few million dollars. Joe paid a high price for what he had. I am sure many would not be willing to pay it if they had the choice.

Loving someone with a spinal cord injury takes everything you have. But they will also teach you what you are made of and show you things about perseverance you didn't know existed.

I am a better person for being Joe's wife. I know I'll never be the same. To be able to tell his story, even with him not being particularly talkative at times, is a great honor. I can only hope I did it a shred of the justice it deserves. God is good. He surely blessed Joe well beyond his expectations.

This book is for anyone who thinks all is lost and life is beyond hope. If you are breathing, God is not done with you yet. Some things in your life might be gone, but that doesn't mean that anything isn't possible from here on. Take up your mat. Trust that God still has good things planned for your life and roll forward. The world is waiting for you to get going.

Chapter 1 - A Troublemaker Is Born

I was born in New Britain, Connecticut, at New Britain General Hospital. It's a small city that you've likely never heard of. Most of the time when people ask where in Connecticut I am from I tell them only to hear, "Where is that?" In case you are wondering, it is exactly two hours in either direction from New York City and Boston. New Britain was the hardware capital of the world at one time. It was home to Stanley tools and many other companies like it. New Britain was a thriving place to grow up in back then. It was a city filled with blue-collar families, all grinding it out in the factories. The downtown streets were filled with the banging of metal and machines making tools. If you saw it today you might have a hard time picturing how that could have been. What was innovation and industry has now been replaced by empty, deteriorating brick shells of the greatness they once were.

My parents were Salvatore and Dolores Paladino. Everyone called my mom "Ceil," short for Celia. She never went by her first name, though I am not sure why. My dad was called "Junior." He was the second in a set of twins. They married young. Most couples married in their late teens in those days. Their first child, a girl, my sister Joyce, came shortly after. I was the first male born in a 100% Sicilian household. This made me the special one. If anyone reading this is Italian, they know what I mean. The first male is the promised child, the one to prize. Ricky came a year and a half later, followed by Steven. We were a house full of rambunctious boys. How my mother didn't lose her mind then I have no idea. A few years later my baby sister, Lisa, came along. Five kids in all in a tiny three-bedroom cape. God bless my parents.

I didn't go to school anywhere special. I went to the local public schools. They were good, as far as public schools go. I walked to school every day with the kids in the neighborhood. Our neighborhood street was lined with neat, modest homes. The square footage a family was raised in back then could hardly constitute a proper home by today's standards. But it was our neighborhood. Neighbors were more like friends. Everyone's parents looked out for the kids that lived around them. Moms spent all day cooking and cleaning for their families. Dads came home smelling of sweat and hard work. We had a big German Shepherd named King. Those were good times.

A neighborhood to a group of boys is like claiming your own turf. Frankie, Bobby, and I spent our weekends playing in the woods. I have great memories of the times we'd build forts out there. These lean-to places were our castles. In there, no one could touch us. The woods were our wonderland full of imagination and possibilities.

I loved my summers with my neighborhood friends, but mom probably needed a break and tried to find something new for us to do. I was introduced to Fresh Air Camp when I was ten. My mom signed me and my little brother, Ricky, up for a couple weeks. Camping in the great outdoors was a big adventure for me and Ricky. I had never been to camp before. One of my favorite experiences was catching lightning bugs in jars and looking at them through the glass. There aren't too many lightning bugs in New Britain. I was fascinated by what they did.

The activities we enjoyed that week were typical of most outdoor camps for kids. We swam in the lake, went canoeing, had bonfires, and lots of other outdoorsy stuff. One thing I didn't like was breakfast: oatmeal. We had oatmeal nearly every single morning. My mom never served oatmeal at home and I saw no reason to start eating it now. Despite the protesting of me and my brother Ricky, oatmeal came to our bowls anyway. When Ricky and I saw no end to oatmeal in sight, we did what only two reasonable kids would do: We decided to run away.

Ricky and I cleverly and carefully planned our oatmeal escape. We'd have to leave when we could evade detection. We'd have to be miles away before anyone knew where we'd gone. Nighttime was the only logical time we could make that happen. We waited for the right night and decided to make a break for it. There was only one problem; the roads were total darkness. To two little kids, walking back roads in the dark is a pretty scary thing. Add in bears and other things that are certain to take you out in the blackness of a forest night and we quickly decided that we'd rather put up with oatmeal than be eaten alive by a hungry bear. Besides, it was going to be a too long a walk to make it home anyway. The oatmeal escape was officially cancelled.

Our mom sent us back the next year but it was clear that going to Fresh Air Camp for two weeks wasn't really our bowl of oatmeal. I wish we'd have taken more advantage of being able to be out in the open during the summer months, but the friends we had in our neighborhood were always there to welcome us back. The world was all right on Bay Avenue. At least it was to us.

When you are really young there are a lot of things you don't notice. Your parents are like the perfect people when you are small, but looking back there was a lot that wasn't quite right. Before we made it to Bay Avenue we lived in my grandparents' three-family apartment house on High Street. Back then it was all Italian families. In fact, despite my mother's parents coming to New Haven, Connecticut, from Sicily some twenty years before, they never really learned English. A lot of people in that neighborhood only spoke Italian. It's all we knew.

What we didn't know, what we couldn't have known then, was the mental health issues my dad had his whole life. Back then no one talked about bipolar depression or any other mental health issue. He was so handsome that he could have been in the movies, maybe on an episode of *The Sopranos*. His bipolar depression produced 'episodes' that would land him in the psych unit of the hospital from time to time. His twin brother had the same problem. With the symptoms came issues with other people. They were always getting into fights. Sometimes they even fought with each other. Mental health issues made it hard for them to get along with each other as well. This put a lot of strain on my dad's family. The issues that belabored his family over the years wouldn't really become evident until years later. While we always had family gatherings for parties in the summer and for the holidays, years of strain took its toll. I didn't see too much of my dad's family after I grew up. Mental health issues that aren't dealt with tend to do that to a family.

Because my dad struggled so much, he had a hard time making money to support his family. We lived paycheck to paycheck with my dad being the only one out there earning money to put food on the table. Not only did my mom not work, as most moms didn't back then, but she never really learned how to read or drive a car. We were totally dependent on my dad being healthy enough to work and the kindness of members of our extended family. Things were a lot more out of balance than they seemed to me as a young boy. Despite it all, my dad managed to do whatever he could to make life good for his kids. I give him a lot of credit. There were plenty of things in his way in life but he somehow managed to make a life for himself and his family. Whatever we wanted he somehow managed to get. One of our biggest surprises was an above ground pool he introduced to our backyard. He also bought me and my brothers minibikes. No matter how modest it was, I am still grateful.

I was always a good student right up until the beginning of my teen years. Why that changed I wish I could put my finger on. It wasn't that I didn't like school, but the kids I was hanging around with in the school yard weren't having any of it. I was introduced to Brian, Mike, and Davie when I was in junior high school. They were the kind of knock-around kids that smoked cigarettes and didn't care about anything. I thought they were cool. Getting in trouble for us was like a rite of passage. How I wished I would have just focused on school and being good. I had no idea back then how much getting into trouble and hanging with the wrong crowd was going to change my life.

Skipping school became a regular occurrence for me after that. So much so that the truant officer had to round me up on a regular basis. When I wouldn't correct my errant ways and ditch my derelict friends, they sent me to reform school.

Getting arrested by the truant officer was a big deal. His name was Mr. Davis. He came to my house one evening to cart me off to juvenile detention. This happened a few times. They'd put in there for a few weeks to try and straighten me out. I felt tough and bad. When you are a kid, you can't appreciate the gravity of what getting yourself into the system really means. Getting sent to juvenile detention can change the trajectory of your life. I couldn't understand the path I was going down but there I was running down it in hopes... of what?

After the third round of being arrested by the truant officer and being sent to juvenile detention didn't work, I was then brought in front of the juvenile court judge. Standing in front of a judge is an intimidating experience. My immaturity prevented me from being able to take it in and be held accountable. I was sentenced to the Connecticut School for Boys in Meriden, CT, for six months.

I remember feeling scared my first day. The school was removed from everyday life in every possible way. I didn't know what to expect, only that my family would visit me at some point. I was issued ugly brown khaki uniforms to wear during my time there. After I got my uniforms, I was escorted to Cottage C. This would be my residence, along with 30 other boys in the same boat as me. Calling the dorms cottages was a bit of a stretch. They were large house-like buildings with three floors. Our meals were served in a separate building. The grounds looked more like what you'd picture an asylum to look like than a school. Aside from the cottages, ominous brick buildings sprawled out into a campus among acres of rolling green grass. We were separated from life alright. Despite the manicured grounds, the length of the front lawn made the statement that no one was welcome to come by unannounced.

I got in a few fights while I was there but everyone was basically okay. It was really hard to get out of line there. I mean, we were already there for being out of line in the first place. No one was going to put up with us.

If you dared to get out of line you were sent to The Hole. That's not what they called it, but that's how us boys referred to it. The Hole is a tiny cell in a separate building where you are subjected to solitary confinement for 24 hrs. The rooms were dark and dank. There was no TV, no nothing. But there was plenty of just sitting and thinking about being in there. I was sad to be sitting by myself. I had already been removed from my tightknit Sicilian family. Being with the other boys in Cottage C gave me some semblance of social interaction. The Hole gave me nothing but me. You'd think that one trip there would have been enough, but my willful pride got the best of me a few times, and to The Hole I went every time.

There were memorable times there too. They had a pool on the grounds that we could use if we were good. Sometimes, I'd get the gumption to behave and be able to take advantage of its spoils. Being able to use the pool made us forget we were forced to be there for just a little while. The water and innocent play made the time at reform school a bit more bearable and life a little more normal.

School work was not allowed to be avoided there. We had to go to class and do our schoolwork. When you are out of the habit of being in school, being forced to participate is pure agony. I thought of my friends at school, the kids in the neighborhood all doing their own things. They were eating home cooked meals made by their moms, and hanging around. There I was in my scratchy brown khaki uniform with a pencil forced in my hand and a blank paper to fill out, face down at my desk. We had some interesting subjects to learn too. They taught us trades like woodworking and automotive. It was probably a good idea to teach us non-school types something we could make a living out of. There's nothing wrong with learning a trade. My mind wasn't really focused on finding a career, though. I mostly just saw it as an opportunity to get out of having to read books and answer questions.

One day, I was in woodworking, cutting wood on the bandsaw. I started the machine and pushed my piece of wood toward the blade. In one split second I became distracted by a noise on the woodshop floor. I pushed as I looked away, unaware that the blade's guard was missing from the machine. My mind was snapped out of the distraction when the blade cut my hand, sending me immediately to the nurse with blood trailing behind.

The school took me to the emergency room where I received several stitches. The cut was so deep that I severed a tendon. While this incident was unfortunate, it also bought me a one-way ticket out of reform school. I was sent home with the reform school's blessing, much to my relief.

You would have thought that reform school would have been enough to scare me straight but it only seemed to embolden me to try more daring things.

One day the following spring, my brother Ricky, my friend Boris and I got the bright idea to hop a Greyhound bus and head to Tampa, FL. There really wasn't any thought-behind plan to do it, we just bought our tickets more or less to dare each other to see if we would go through with it. The next day we were there in sunny Florida for the first time in our lives. We had eight dollars among the three of us, and not one stitch of clothing besides what was on our backs. We had no idea where we would stay or where our next meal would come from, but we were excited to be there.

We had a great time that day, walking the beach and taking in the sites. Swaying palm trees brushed the sky and waved hello to us. The sun kissed our New England faces. The warm breeze made all seem right in the world. That is until it became clear that our perfect day turned into an uncertain night. We had nowhere to stay and even if we had enough money, no hotel would rent a room to three young teenage boys. We decided to sleep in the bathroom at the bus station, but that plan was rudely interrupted by the Tampa police who arrested us for loitering and promptly dropped us off at a home for runaway teens. That wasn't in the big plans we had for our adventure in Florida.

The police got in touch with my parents who sent money for bus tickets home. Just as soon as we arrived, we were turned right around. I wish my parents would have laid down the law, and given it to me good for that. But aside from being visibly upset when I saw them, that was it for punishments. Had they been stricter, it might have made a difference. With no direction and no discipline, I made up my mind that I could do whatever I wanted.

The summer didn't prove to be any better step in the right direction. Being bored with the neighborhood and not wanting to be around my parents, I decided to hitchhike to the local shoreline with my friend, Pete. It was about an hour by car, too long to walk. Everyone hitchhiked then anyway. We soon arrived at Sound View in Connecticut, a small boardwalk on the beach with ice cream shops, burger stands, and a merry-go-round. It had everything a young teen boy could want in a beach destination. And it had girls in bikinis there.

The first girl to catch my eye was Debbie. She was a pretty, skinny blonde with blue eyes and a sweet smile. I walked up to her at the arcade. I tried to say something funny, but I wasn't that smooth. She thought I was cute and so I followed her around with her friends for the rest of the day. The reward for my efforts for getting myself down to the beach without permission was Debbie. I was smitten.

As the day wore on Pete was getting nervous about his parents and getting into trouble. I didn't care. Pete called his parents on a payphone to tell them where we were. A couple hours later, Pete's parents came down to Sound View to grab him by the scruff of the neck and cart him off back home. I watched the whole thing go down right there on the side of the road, hidden behind a house. I wasn't going back to New Britain for anything. When my parents realized they weren't going to find me, they went back home with Pete and his parents.

I found Debbie and her friends again and relaxed knowing my night there was safe. I had nowhere to stay and no money for anything, but that didn't seem to matter with Debbie around. I decided she was going to be my girlfriend for the summer. Sound View was going to be my new home as far as I was concerned. We walked around the boardwalk with her friends all day. With Pete back home, I didn't have to worry about anyone else ruining my vagabond vacation plans.

The sun started to set over the water and I had to say goodnight to Debbie. It was time for her to go back to her family's beach cottage and I tried to make it seem like I had somewhere to go, too. After a sweet little kiss goodbye, with a little giggle from her friends nearby, Debbie went home and I found a spot to sleep on the beach with an empty stomach.

The next morning, I shook off the sand and tried to smooth my hair down with my hands and try to look like I had it together. I wanted to find Debbie again. But I also needed to eat. The realization I had no food made me start planning for how I was going to find what I needed to survive. I found Debbie later that morning and told her I had nothing to eat. She and her friends took pity on me and decided to get me some food. I could trust the girls to come through for me when I needed food or money. Not a bad gig for a homeless kid on the beach.

Debbie and I were an item that summer. This was something her father wasn't too keen on. Turns out he had something against his daughter hanging around some ragamuffin she found at the arcade. He was a successful man who owned a well-known construction company. He had better plans for his daughter's suitor than the likes of me. Debbie and I kept our relationship away from the judgmental eyes of her dad after that. Little did he know that at night, when he was asleep, his daughter used to hide me under her bed. She'd get me up early in the morning and toss me out to the beach before her dad had a chance to realize I was there.

When I decided I was going to be staying more than a few weeks, I found a local burger joint looking for summer help. It was a campy beach restaurant. Just the kind you'd find on a boardwalk with sunburned kids and their tired parents crowded around a booth eating fried food and shaking the sand off their feet.

The owner felt bad for me when I explained my situation. He agreed that I could come and flip burgers at night in exchange for a small amount of pay and a spot to sleep in the storage room upstairs. I got to eat when I worked and had a couple of dollars in my pocket for the arcade and Debbie. It was nice to be able to buy her an ice cream and hold her hand while we walked. She was the only normal thing in my life that summer. People aren't normally sleeping in storage rooms and swimming in the ocean for a bath. Everything was going great until the owner's wife got wind that a runaway teenage boy was sleeping in her restaurant at night. After that, I'd have to make other sleeping arrangements. I thanked the owner anyway and never went back.

My situation was getting a little dicey. I had nowhere to sleep and no more income. I was wandering around the beach the next night, trying to figure out what to do next. Debbie wasn't around so I didn't have any bed to sleep under that night. I was looking for something to do when I rounded a street corner to hear a guy's voice pouring out of a microphone and onto the street. He was a crooner if ever there was one. He was the Saturday night entertainment at the beach nightclub. I went around to the back of the club to find the back door wide open. I found a wooden produce box to sit on and took in the music. It was a nice break from the stress of trying to figure out what to do with myself.

I stayed out there watching bartenders and waitstaff take turns coming out for some air and a smoke. No one bothered me sitting on the box. I am sure I wasn't the only bored kid that showed up back there. After the night was done the crooner with the Dean Martin voice came out to start loading his stuff into his car. He saw me sitting out there and told me he'd give me five bucks if I'd help him get his stuff out of the club and put it into his trunk. I shrugged and got up to help. Why not? I was happy to have money for food the next morning.

He said his name was Dino Minelli. From the look of it, he seemed like a bigshot. Guys with their dates kept coming up to him to tell him how great he was. Everyone kept shaking his hand and slapping him on back. I was hanging around behind everyone waiting for him to tell me what to do. When the crowd finally dispersed he found me waiting and we got to work packing him up for the night.

While we were walking from the club to his car with all his stuff, he asked me what I was doing out there. I told him about my adventure on the beach for the summer and said since I was kicked out of my impromptu room at the burger joint, I had no more job and nowhere else to go. He told me he was sorry for the tough break and asked me if I'd like to sleep on his front porch that night. Seeing as I had no other offers, I told him that would be fine. We drove to his summer home and he pointed to a wicker couch as we came in the porch door. He fetched me a blanket from the house and handed it to me and told me to sleep well.

The next morning he let me shower and I got a better look at him and his beach house. It was a little ratty summer house just off the beach. He and his family were staying there while he was singing for the summer. He was a handsome man. He had wavy dark brown hair that was neatly kept but a little grown out. It was a typical hairstyle for an older man in the 1970s.

Once he got dressed, he asked me if I would come to the grocery store with him to get a carton of cigarettes. We backed out of the driveway toward the store and he started asking me questions about why I was down in Sound View without my family and what I had been up to since I got there. I wasn't sure if he was just curious or he was thinking of figuring out how to call my parents but I felt obligated to answer him since he let me stay for the night. He asked me if I wanted a job being his errand boy while he was down there. He also said he could probably get me some odd jobs for a couple of bucks here and there. I said that would be great, but I still needed somewhere to sleep. He said I could stay on the porch if I wanted. I agreed. It wasn't the best place to make home but it was better than sleeping on the beach or some car on the side of the road with its doors unlocked.

When we got back to his place he handed me a couple of bucks and a pack of cigarettes and told me to come find him at the club around 4 P.M. to help him get set up. I was happy to be a little more settled.

I caught up with Debbie later on that morning at the arcade. I told her about my new friend Dino and that he would get me some work. I told her I could stay on his porch so I wouldn't need her to hide me at her house. She was relieved. My life was falling into place down the beach. Well, at least as far as I could make it.

My summer on the beach was one of the best memories I have of my teen years. Being Dino's righthand man made me feel special and cared for. I met so many people hanging around Dino. Debbie was the dream girl from the beach. But just like all summers end, so did my relationship with Debbie. All I have to remember her by is the tattoo I got of her name on my wrist.

Chapter 2 – A Bad Moon Is Rising

When the beach became quiet as the summer wound down, I went back home to New Britain. My parents were relieved to find me in one piece. I promised to never run away to the beach again, even though we all knew I wasn't good with keeping promises to be good. I got yelled at plenty but no punishments were assigned. It was good to have my own bed to sleep in and a homecooked meal from my mom's kitchen. I missed her cooking.

While I was gone, my cousin Cindy started coming around with her boyfriend Dave to visit my parents a lot. My parents were the kind of people that everyone liked being around. My dad was jovial and hospitable when people visited and my mom liked to talk to anyone who was up for a conversation. I sat down with them all one night to find out what the gossip was with the family and see who this guy was hanging out with my parents in our kitchen.

I watched Dave as he talked. He had a swagger, a confidence about him. He was the kind of guy who ran any room he was in. I wanted to be like that. When he spoke, people shut up and listened.

I found out a couple days later from my cousin Cindy that Dave was in a street gang called THE EARLS. I didn't know anyone in something like that. I had my suspicions that some of my singing friend Dino's friends were in the mob, but I never had a real gang member in my kitchen before. Dave was cool. I wanted to be just like him.

THE EARLS was just a high school club in the 1950s. They had varsity-style football jackets for their club jackets. They were black wool with white sleeves. Their jackets had a pink E where a high school emblem would be. But the 1950s turned into the 60s and everybody changed then. With the culture changes of the 60s came a personality shift to a street gang. THE EARLS was a full-fledged street gang by 1970. The gang uniform now included a black leather vest with the gang colors and patches. It was something more fitting to go with the edgier attitude of the club.

Just about that time a kid on my street name Jimmy joined THE EARLS too. He was ten years older than me but I hang out with him sometimes. We'd hang out in front of his house, smoke cigarettes and shoot the breeze. Jimmy always had thoughts on the things going on around him. He was good to talk to when you wanted to feel a little smarter for a 14-year-old kid. Jimmy said I was too young to join. The minimum age requirement to be an EARL was 16. It was a bummer but that's just the way it was. Jimmy thought I ought to focus on other things besides gang membership.

It was okay I was too young for THE EARLS. I had more enterprising things to do, like lifting car stereos and bikes with my friend Tony. I met Tony when my older sister Joyce started dating him in middle school. They didn't last too long but he and I got to be good buddies. Besides, we had petty theft in common so he made a good ally. When you are a teen boy up to no good, you find others just like you. Tony and I were a master thieving duo together.

When I wasn't out lifting cars, I started taking an interest in pool halls. It was fun to walk by them and see the guys leaning over pool tables with cigarettes hanging out of their mouths. The focus was on the shooter as they rest of them would stand, leaning on pool sticks while they waited for the outcome of the move. The smell of beer and stale smoke would waft out the door as I'd peer in until I was shewed away by the bar manager.

There was one hall I peered into on a regular basis. I must have worn down the barkeep because one day I stood in the doorway, leaning on the doorjamb like I was holding up the wall. One of the guys at one of the tables waived me over to his game. He was a potbellied polish guy with a thick accent and a scruffy face. His hands were big and meaty from working at the hardware factories. He asked me if I knew how to play. I shrugged and shook my head. He said, "Come let me show you how. You can play for money if you get good enough." He chuckled along with the other guys standing around. I heard the word *money* and that is all I needed. This I could do.

The game wasn't as easy as it looked but the man was patient. He finally got around to telling me his name was Peter, when it occurred to him that he didn't know what to call me. Peter and I met up on most days when I skipped school, which was pretty often. He taught me the game long enough for me to get good and a little full of myself. After a couple weeks I asked Peter when I could play for money like him and his friends did.

A couple of guys overheard us and took me up on a paid game. I think they were thinking they could roll the cocky kid for a couple of dollars and teach me a lesson. I slapped my money down on the pool table and told them I'd have a go. I didn't win that game but it burned me good. I played pool with Peter as much as I could until he told me I was ready.

When the time came around to ask if I could get in on a paid game, the guys had seen me playing with Peter and they knew I could hold my own. This time I had some respect from the guys around the pool hall, even if they usually complained to me that I should be in school, not hanging out with the likes of them. The next paid game I won, and then I won again. I walked out of that pool hall that day with 20 dollars. I was hooked. Between stealing car stereos, bikes and being a pool shark, I was never without money in my pocket. It kept me occupied by it didn't keep me out of the police station.

Months later, THE EARLS started getting to be a big thing in New Britain. Jimmy told me it had gotten up to over 50 members one day when I saw him out on his porch. Everyone was talking about THE EARLS. They were the cool guys everybody was looking up to.

THE EARLS also had their rivals. THE LORDS was their arch rival gang. When THE EARLS and THE LORDS showed up at the same place anything could happen at the drop of a cigarette butt. Fist fights were usually the end to a run in with each other. There were a handful of other gangs in town, but THE EARLS and THE LORDS were the two biggest. THE EARLS sometimes got into it with a motorcycle gang called The Drifters, but it wasn't anything like the animosity towards THE LORDS.

Tony was a year older than me so I was surprised and thrilled to hear he was pledging for THE EARLS one afternoon when we met up for an evening of car stereo heisting. I wanted to know all about how to join but I was still too young. Tony, being my friend, agreed to bring me around. I asked Dave about it one night and he thought it'd be okay if I hung around with them sometimes as long as I was with Dave and Tony.

The thought of being in with the cool guys, the tough kids, made me swell with pride. They were somebody and I wanted to be somebody people respected too. Wearing THE EARLS colors meant you belonged. It meant you couldn't be messed with. It meant someone had your back. They called each other brothers and man, I wanted to be with a group of guys who were that close too.

The first time Dave and Tony brought me to an EARLS keg party was exciting. The testosterone in the house was high and pretty girls were everywhere you looked. All the cool girls wanted to date an EARL. Being in that environment was intoxicating, never mind the beer. A street gang is an attractive option for a lost kid looking to make his mark on the world. I didn't like school, I had no real hobbies and no one at home making sure I wasn't steered in the right direction. I was the perfect profile of a street gang candidate.

I decided that my goal in life would be to become and EARL. It was all I could think about. I was jealous that Tony was already in THE EARLS but I still hung around the club a lot. The idea of being part of a brotherhood was the common theme that brought all the guys together. To them, brotherhood was everything. When you were an EARL, you were it for everything. Your club brothers came before everything else. All you heard about what the importance of seeing these guys as your brothers. In gang life, your club brothers were your family and everything came after them.

My old friends from the neighborhood didn't matter to me any more if they didn't want to be in the club. I wasn't interested in teen things any more. I wanted to be a man that belonged to a community that had my back and thought of me as family. When you want to belong, this is a powerful thing to become drawn to. I wish I never got involved with the club. My life would have turned out so much differently. My parents never wanted me to be part of the club. They wanted me to go to school and be a normal kid. I wished I'd listened to them and stayed in school. It just didn't go that way.

The club had clubhouses but they were really just rented apartments. Some of the guys would clean up and get dressed in suits to look at apartments. Once the landlord thought they were clean-cut guys with jobs, they'd rent to them. After that the club would move and before you knew it, music, weed smoke and people were hanging out the windows partying at all hours of the day and night. It wouldn't take too long before the club would get thrown out an apartment and they'd have to find one all over again.

The parties, the girls, the whole thing; I wanted it all. I wanted the vest and colors that said I belonged. When I wasn't doing anything else, I was at the club. I was what they call a hang-around. I couldn't belong but I was there with THE EARLS all the time. I wanted to be such a fixture to them that they couldn't think of saying no when it was time for me to pledge for membership.

My sister Joyce had the nerve to date one of the LORDS when I was hanging out with THE EARLS. This would have been a great insult but I wasn't a member yet and Joyce wasn't really interested in what I thought about her boyfriends any way. Sometimes I'd go hang out with her when she hung out with the LORDS. I didn't tell any of THE EARLS, though. I didn't want to ruin my chances of getting in. They were pretty cool guys, though. When Joyce got tired of dating one of the LORDS she met Gene. He was in THE EARLS so my conflict of interest was eliminated. I was relieved.

Gangs back then weren't like what they are today. We weren't into selling drugs or guns or anything like that. We liked to hang around and party. The motorcycle gangs were around but that wasn't us. Some of our members had bikes but we weren't anything like the what you'd think of when it comes to a motorcycle gang. Some of the members wanted to become a motorcycle gang once but that was shot down by the other members pretty quickly.

Being a hang-around had its perks, but it also had its consequences. I knew a lot about what THE EARLS got themselves into. That made me have to keep secrets. Some of them were secrets I wish I never had to keep. Things happened at the parties sometimes that were not good. With a lot of guys and drinking, things can get out of hand quickly.

Some of the girls we hung out with shouldn't have been there so late into the night. A couple of times things got pretty wild and there were plenty of rumors about some of the guys going around town.

These were the secrets I had to keep as a club hang-around. No matter what, the club came first. And no matter what anyone did, I was sworn to secrecy. Some of those secrets I still live with.

My time to pledge was drawing nearer and I was more excited about being a real member. I wanted to shed my hang-around title and put on my EARLS vest and colors more than anything. I was totally submerged in the gang life by then. My family knew I was totally given over to this lifestyle and there was nothing they could do about it. What my parents must have said to each other about it, I can only imagine. I feel sad when I think of how much it must have hurt them but at the time I didn't care about anything else.

I wanted to behave myself with the club brothers to make sure I was on their good side. I didn't want anyone to have a reason to not let me in the club. Tony was my best friend so I knew I had him on my side. Jimmy was a good friend, too. I had no reason to think he didn't want me in the club, so that was two. Dave was a bigshot in the club so I thought I could count on him. I just had to wait for my time.

I wish I could tell you that I did whatever other kid my age did at 15. I could have been mowing lawns for extra money or worked at the supermarket. Instead I stole whatever I could and sold it for cash. I was well-known to the police for my stealing antics but they couldn't do anything because I was a juvenile. I was never formally arrested for anything I did because I was just a kid. Kids didn't get arrested then. Sometimes I wish I did. Maybe I would have gotten straightened out. My sister was all about dating guys in clubs, too. This was the life the kids in my town were in.

Finally, old enough to pledge. Only an official club brother for THE EARLS could make it happen. Thankfully, my friend Tony was the one who brought me up at a club meeting to pledge for membership. If I didn't love him before, I loved him then. I thought the day would never come.

The club meeting was held for pledges. The meetings were held in the park to add to the mystery. At this kind of meeting, everyone stands in a circle and you walk in and around everyone and then you stand like a man and let them ask you questions. I had been hanging around these guys all this time, but today I felt like they were all new to me. I was about to find out what they really thought of me. They asked me all the usual questions. It was nothing too complicated, just questions from different guys about why I wanted to join. The questioning was a blur. Before I had a chance to really think about it, I was dismissed from the group so the voting could begin. You couldn't be present for the vote. You'd never know who voted for you and who didn't, just whether you got in or not. When the circle broke up, I was told I could pledge.

The time for pledges to prove themselves worthy of membership lasted two weeks. I had to do whatever any member asked me to do. I wasn't supposed refuse anything from anyone who was a member. I'd been hanging around these guys for years though. Every time I was asked to do something I wanted to laugh at them, but I played along with the game. I wanted to be official so I had to do what I needed to so I could wear my colors.

One of the things pledges are typically asked to do is wash the bikes of the members. You'd be asked to wash motorcycles and make them shine. It was stupid, mindless stuff but it made the members feel important and make the pledges know where their place was. There I was, washing and polishing motorcycles for some of my friends. It was probably the most genuine work I'd ever done, to be honest.

It was typical to go to parties on weekends. Saturday night was the big night for partying. Between our own parties and parties we heard about through the grapevine, there was a lot of drinking and driving. Back then people didn't take it too seriously, like they do today. We'd all pile into cars and head off in a caravan to our destination. We'd hang out there until we got bored and pile into cars again to the next party. I was two weeks away from being an official member. As far as I was concerned, I was already a member, I just had to wait for my pledge time to be up. It was a time to relax and enjoy my life. I saw a future with THE EARLS as what I always wanted. I was almost 16 and my life was exactly the way that I wanted it. Just like every teen my age, I felt like I was untouchable.

Chapter 3 – Accidents Happen

The weekend of my birthday was just like all the others. We had party after party lined up that Saturday night. Our first stop was at a keg party at a park that evening. It was just one of the stops. We went to the first party and drank our fill of cheap beer. A couple hours after we decided that the party at Stanley Quarter Park across town would be more fun. This party was in the woods. We'd take the cars over to the park and drive down the dark park roads to our destination. We'd gone to parties in the woods there all the time.

There was no reason to think this night would be any different. Just like most guys who have a few drinks, there was joking and jesting as we were getting into the cars. The challenge of a race to our destination was made and of course the challenge was accepted. I hopped in the passenger's side of Bob's car and two girls we were with piled into the back. In a split second we were off and running, careening to our next party.

Two cars barreled toward Stanley Quarter Park. I was in the car in the lead. We flew through the entrance of the park with our friends coming up close behind. On the other side of the park was the dark park road we needed to take to get to the keg party waiting for us in the woods. The road was unlit and windy. We'd been down this road so many times before. The thought to be careful never entered anyone's mind as the engine revved and all had a good time laughing and looking back to see where the car behind us was.

The car leaned and flew rocks as we sped around corners. This corner was the tightest, I took one look back to see how far we were in the lead. As I turned back around to look ahead I saw the tree. We were head on for a collision. No one had any time to react. Before I could even brace myself I felt my body slide out from under me.

I blacked out on impact. I tried to come around but my mind was foggy and I couldn't understand what anyone was saying. I didn't even know I was wedged under the dashboard of Bob's car. It occurred to me to move but I couldn't. Everything felt numb. I realized my arm was stuck underneath the front seat. I still couldn't say anything. The partygoers in the woods must have heard the crash. I remember hearing voices all around the car but I didn't recognize them.

What I know now was that the party came running up to the scene to see me stuck in Bob's car. Everyone was screaming for someone to get help. A few minutes later, the police came with their cop ambulance. It wasn't the kind of ambulances you see today. It wasn't a painted up van with lots of lights. It was a black station wagon and it was the police who took you to the hospital then. I became aware of what was happening when I heard the police surveying the situation of me crumbled up under the dashboard. I could hear them asking questions and getting equipment near me to get me out. I was wondering how I was going to get out of there because I couldn't move anything. Helplessly, I awaited rescue.

"You're not so tough now, are you, Joe?" I heard that come from one of the cops who was helping me. I don't know who it was but in the situation I was in, it was hardly what I needed to hear.

I felt them put the rescue collar around my neck just seconds before they hoisted my motionless body out of the car and onto the nearby stretcher. I faded in and out on the way to the hospital. I don't recall much about it. My situation came into full view in the emergency room. My parents were already there, along with most of my club brothers. They were circling around me, talking to me. My Uncle Guy was there. He got a good look at me and asked, "Why are your eyes all red?" That's all I remember before things went fuzzy again.

The next thing I knew I was in the operating room. I came to again to the sound of a voice saying to the operating room staff, "Careful, I don't want to kill him." I had awakened in the middle of my operation. I needed more anesthesia. I went out again, thankfully.

After my operation, they moved me to the ICU. I awoke to my motionless body and a halo around my head. My head was completely immobilized with screws fastened to my head so I wouldn't move. That's when I got the news from the doctor. I had broken my neck at C6 and C7. A fusion was necessary to fix my neck into place. I had an operation to do that. My spinal cord was pinched when I broke it. That is why I couldn't move anything.

I had no time to panic because my club brothers were there, all gathered around me. I had woken up in time for the good news. I made the club. I was officially an EARL and that is all that I cared about. I had no idea of the gravity of my situation. I was paralyzed and almost totally motionless, but I didn't care because I was a gang member. I count it a blessing that I was so young when I got injured for one reason, I didn't appreciate what life would be like from here on out. The foolishness of youth kept me from focusing on my situation and on the fact that I was part of a community of derelicts with no direction in life and no sense of right living.

I was going to be in the hospital for quite a while. I was going nowhere anyway in the condition I was in. I didn't like being stuck in one place, not mention I was frozen in one position with my paralysis and a halo keeping my head still. The nurses had to flip me to keep me from getting bed sores, an exercise I hated having to go through. I wanted to get up. I wanted to go home. I didn't want to be in the hospital. The longer I stayed the more miserable I was to be around. My poor terrified parents came to visit me and stayed every night until visitors' hours ended at 10 P.M. I soured over the constant consoling by them. I admit, they bore the brunt of my frustration on more than one night. I'd feel bad when they'd leave heartbroken, but I wanted out of there. They were just a reminder of what happened to me and I didn't want to think about it. My grandmother, Nunna, came to visit me every day. She didn't really speak English but that didn't stop her from being a regular presence at the hospital. She'd come and try to get me to eat, but I wasn't really hungry. Most of the time she'd end up eating what was on my tray instead. What we didn't get to say with words, we made up in just being together. I knew she cared. She didn't have to figure out how to say it.

My only source of happiness is when my club brothers would come visit me. They'd crowd into my room, as many as would fit in there. The nurses became agitated over the sight of them coming down the hallway. One night they came and hung my new vest with my club colors over my bed, a sight none of the hospital staff appreciated but it made me feel like more of an EARL. I certainly wasn't a tough guy trapped in a hospital bed with no way to do anything. The group of them would usually stay until security or the police were called to remove them. It made me feel like I belonged to have them make such a big deal over visiting me.

The doctor overseeing my care came in one day and told me I had to start physical therapy. They were going to see if they could stand me up using some apparatus. I wasn't too excited to give it a try and less so when I went to therapy the first time and they strapped me to a flat table to try and get me into an erect position. It was no use, I wasn't bearing weight or moving anything. I just wanted to be left alone after that but they insisted I keep going. Over the next couple of weeks my arms started to move again. That fueled my desire to get physical with the hospital staff when I felt like resisting therapy. I wasn't really up for the task of fighting orderlies but it didn't stop me from trying. The more I was made to do things the angrier I got. *Why won't they just leave me alone?* I thought. *I want to get out of here.*

If I could have left, I would have. But my body wouldn't cooperate so New Britain General is where I called home for the next two months. Halfway through my stay at New Britain General, the halo on my head came off. I was so relieved to get those painful screws out of my head. The doctors fitted me with a fancy neck brace. It was the best in technology at the time.

After two months New Britain General did all they could do. The medical team thought it was best if I went to Newington Children's Hospital for further rehabilitation. There wasn't much to rehabilitate. I wondered why anyone thought they should try. I could move my arms, but my hands wouldn't work. Standing me up wasn't happening. I couldn't even move a toe if someone paid me a million dollars. I just wanted to go home. I didn't know what the point was of going but I had no choice.

I got settled into Newington Children's Hospital. This is where they started getting me used to a wheelchair. I hadn't been in one since I got hurt but I needed to get oriented to how to use one. The doctor at Newington Children's was the one to break it to me and my parents that I would never walk again.

I think when you get injured so young, you have a tendency to deny what is the truth. Somewhere in my mind I wanted him to be wrong. But no matter what I thought about it, I had to learn how to get around. The wheelchair was my ticket mobility so I looked at it as the thing that could get me out the hospital.

The hospital staff tried as hard as they could to rally me around to the idea of putting the effort into my rehabilitation but I couldn't have cared less. I wanted to be with my club brothers doing what we did before. I wanted to be a carefree sixteen-year-old kid again. My club brothers poured into the hospital almost daily. They drove the nurses and hospital staff nuts there. I loved to see them come barreling into my room, laughing and joking. They wanted to cheer me up, I loved that about them. They proudly rehung my club colors in my room, as a reminder of what was waiting for me when I got out.

When my club brothers weren't there I was bored and restless. I got used to getting around in a wheelchair so I started wheeling around the hospital when I could. That wheeling around brought me to meet a girl named Miriam. She was on the same floor as me. She had scoliosis so she was there recovering from a back surgery. She was a pretty Italian girl with light olive skin, long dark hair. She was stuck in her room in a body cast from the neck down. I decided to go visit her when I could. It made us both feel better to have a friend in there. Besides, what teenage boy doesn't want to take an opportunity to chat it up with a pretty girl?

Miriam and I talked about all kinds of things. Frankly, we had the time. We'd hold hands and talk about all that we were missing out on and what it was like to be stuck in there.

Our friendship also brought some camaraderie to our parents. I am sure that having kids laid up in a rehab hospital was hard. They came together as Italians and as parents who were trying not to worry so much about their kids. Miriam and her family were from Poughkeepsie, NY, so her parents traveled a long way to see their daughter. My parents spent a lot of time talking to them when they came to visit at the same time. My best memories of that time were of Miriam's friendship and seeing my parents relax a little around their new friends. I wanted to get out of there so bad, but I also wanted to stay for Miriam. I think she is what made me want to give recovering more of a go than I had before.

Since I was sort of being good, the hospital let me go home for the day on the weekends sometimes. I'd get to go to my house for a few hours. I had to travel on a big tilt wheelchair with a high back. The wheelchair took up a lot of room and I still had my neck brace so I was quite presence in the small kitchen of my parent's house. Friends and family would come and visit. It was great to feel a little normal for a the time I was there.

One weekend, I got to go on a visit for a night. It was around Christmas and my club brothers and my dad picked me up and took me to THE EARLS Christmas party. I felt like I was on cloud nine to be around my club brothers having a great time. I hadn't been to a celebration since my accident. We laughed and enjoyed the visit, but all too soon, I had to go back to the rehab and go to bed in my hospital room. I had so much fun that night but it made me even more homesick to have to go back to the rehab all alone. *Will I ever get out of here?*

The weeks turned into months that seemed like years. I was stuck somewhere I didn't want to be and no way to get to where I wanted to go. The hum of the hospital wore on my nerves. I didn't want people constantly caring for me. I resented their help. I wanted to be left alone and go be an EARL. I wondered when the magic day would come, that I'd get to leave but the nurses and occupational therapists I talked to didn't have any answers. They just wanted me to focus on my recovery. What recovery?

The doctors me and my parents met with when I got there didn't have any hope that I'd regain the use of my legs. I still couldn't close my hands or move my fingers. What did they expect for recovery? All of it seemed pointless to me. Recovery stood in the way of me hanging with the club and just feeling like I was in control of my own life again.

The guys in the club came to visit all the time but I didn't want to hang with them in the hospital. No one in the hospital wanted them there when they came anyway. It was always tense having to deal with upset nurses and hostile security hovering around while they were there.

I would have dreams in my sleep that I was still walking. In every dream there was no wheelchair. I could run, ride a bike, and kick a ball. In my dreams I could still feel what it felt like to kick a ball. In reality,

I couldn't even feel my feet never mind kick anything. I'd wake up disappointed to be back in the body that wouldn't move. Only in my dreams was I a normal kid. In real life I was a captive in a motionless body. I wanted to be paroled.

Chapter 4 – The Road Back Home

Finally, the day came when the hospital staff decided there was no more progress to be made. Besides, I wasn't even a willing participant in rehab on most days. I would be going back to my parents' house to try and pick up the pieces of my life and what was left of my 16th year.

I am sure my parents were nervous to have me there. My mom would be my nurse and my caregiver. I am sure it felt a lot like having a new baby home for the first time. No one knew what to expect even when they were told what to do. Doing life in a wheelchair was all new to us. No matter what we faced, I knew it would be better than being stuck in the hospital. I was willing to deal with whatever headaches came with my discharge back into life.

My parents set up my room in the den. It was the only room that I could get to and had enough room for me and everyone to move around in with my chair. I had a regular bed to sleep in. Back then there were no special beds with fancy mattresses for people like me. It wasn't perfect but it was the best that my parents could do for me.

A nurse came for a couple months to help my mom acclimate to being able to care for me. I had a foley catheter in place so that had to be checked on for infections and stuff. I couldn't get into the bathroom for a shower so my mom had to sponge bathe me. I burned with humiliation over my mom having to wash me so I quickly figured out how I could wash myself.

Dressing was an obstacle I'd have to learn to jump over. I challenge anyone to try and dress yourself without standing up or moving your legs. Oh, and don't grip anything you put on either. It's not as easy as it looks. I had to figure out how to do it. My mom and I clumsily got the hang of how to dress me in under 20 minutes.

The nervousness of everything being new wore off and the house settled into a new routine. Family is that way. It's the Italian way. When one has a problem in the family, we all have a problem. We put our minds to getting things to feel normal and we made it happen.

Once I was settled into my life as a quadriplegic, I got back to wanting to be with my club brothers. They'd drive up in a car to get me and they'd haul me out of my house, chair and all. I probably had no business being carted around by a bunch of hooligans but this is the life I was looking forward to the whole time I was in the hospital. Being out with them made me feel free, like I could be okay. They accepted me just the way I was and they were with me the whole time I was in the hospital. Why would I not want to be with them?

The thing that got in the way of life as a teenage kids was the sweating. I'd sweat through shirts constantly. I was always cold because I was sweating so much. There was nothing I could do about it. It was side-effect of my spinal cord injury. I prayed for this sweating to go away, but it went on relentlessly, despite my distress over it at times.

One dumb thing I did with my club brothers was go on a weekend adventure to Hampton Beach, NH, with them. My family thought it would be a great idea for me to go. I was foolish to think they could care for me. My dad and mom loved them so they didn't mind that I went. I was picked up and put in the car by the guys and off to the New Hampshire coastline we went.

The club rented a cottage and 20 of us were in it. The partying ensued and went nonstop the whole time. Alcohol and weed were everywhere, along with all kinds of girls. The girls came in and out of the cottage. It was like watching them in a parade. I tried to have fun and let go a little but it was hard to watch guys being guys and not being able to participate the way I wanted to.

One carload of guys came with three butchered pigs to roast while we were there. It was a bizarre display of three dead pigs dressed up in jackets with THE EARLS' colors. They cooked them and ate them, hacking off pieces to eat all weekend. The site of it turned my stomach. There were so many people in the cottage that I was fixed in place in my chair all weekend. These kinds of situations aren't good for people in chairs. I had a feeling I didn't make the right decision by going, but alcohol and smoking weed cured my second thoughts.

Thankfully, the weekend was over and they took me home to the comfort and safety of my parents' house. My mom and dad were anxious to hear if I had a good time. I was glad for home-cooked meals and a clean bed to sleep in.

Being a kid going through something like this wasn't helping me get better. Instead of dealing with the fact that my loose and fast life was the reason I was in a wheelchair, I went full steam ahead on my gang life. Whenever the guys came to get me I went with them. It was the usual routine of a couple guys carrying me out of the house, chair and all, and putting me in a car to go with them. It didn't occur to me that being around them was detrimental to my life. I didn't care. Besides, my dad loved to have them around. What my parents were thinking for encouraging me to hang out with a gang, I don't know. Looking back, they made the wrong decision, but I was glad they didn't give me a hard time. The club was going to be my life, quad life or not.

I was very dependent on people for the things that I needed still and these guys weren't careful about anything. They had the same philosophy on life I had: living for today only. What did I have anyway? I quit school just before I got hurt so I didn't have that to go back to. I had no job or any career prospects before I wound up in a chair, so I didn't consider what my financial future would be like. I didn't have a girlfriend and I didn't think any girl would want to date a guy like me anyway. All I had was this group of losers. They stood by me no matter what and I was going to do the same for them, even if I couldn't actually stand.

The club got an apartment they called the clubhouse. It was where we hung out as an official gang headquarters. The guys would hall me all the way up to the third floor where the apartment was, chair and all. It was exciting to be with all the guys at the clubhouse. We had some wild parties in that place. Girls, girls, girls, and more booze than you could imagine.

I loved being at the clubhouse so much that I started staying there. My parents didn't seem to mind and they knew it wouldn't matter if they did. I needed care and looking after but I was too prideful to admit it. I wanted to be the tough guy who could get through this on my own. The problem was, the guys didn't know how to take care of me. I was too self-conscious to ask for what I needed. Most of the time everyone was too drunk or high to do anything for me anyway. It was a recipe for disaster.

I started to decline from lack of care. I was stationed on the couch when I wasn't in my chair and being in one spot for any length of time isn't good for anyone with paralysis. The constant drinking with my club brothers was out of control. Most days and nights I'd pass out on the couch, drunk. After prolonged neglect and abuse to my body over the course of the year, it started breaking down. My first pressure sores started materializing on my hips from being stuck in one position and being too drunk to care about it. I got one pressure sore on each hip at the same time. For walking people, when their bodies get uncomfortable from being in the same position their nerves tell their bodies to move so the blood can recirculate to the areas that have had constant pressure for too long. For people like me, we never get that message to the brain that says, "Move." Being intoxicated all the time was making my body reject my lifestyle. Pressure sores formed on my feet as well.

I tried to ignore my pressure sores and take care of them myself. My body was becoming a mess. I was a mess. My life was a mess. You would think that would be enough to decide this life wasn't for me any longer but I persisted. I remained committed to my ignorant lifestyle until I wound up in the hospital for infections due to my pressure sores. The neglect of my body cost me five months in the hospital. It was a blessing in disguise. Despite my anguish over being in the hospital again and being away from the club, I needed to dry out so my body could heal. Being in the club was affecting my health, even to the point of risking my life, but I wouldn't even consider not being an EARL.

One day my club brothers came in for a visit with a quart of vodka. We were all joking and passing it around until a nurse came in and caught us. The guys were promptly thrown out of the hospital. We never took anything seriously and when they could manage to get in, they came to see me. Most of the time, they didn't manage to get in with the vodka.

I was discharged from the hospital finally when the sores closed and I looked healthy again and it was right back to the life I had before. I had no appreciation for the precious value of my life.

I became interested in getting tattoos. Tattoos were popular around the tough guys, they always were. My club brothers were clocking a lot of hours at tattoo parlors and I went with them. Back then you didn't come in the door with a drawing and expect some tattoo artist to do it like you do today. In those days you pointed to a drawing on the wall and said, "I'll have that."

Getting tattoos made me feel like a man and like I was one of the guys. Tattoo parlors back then had no health code standards. People drank and smoked in tattoo parlors. They were filthy establishments but no one cared. The only thing that mattered was getting one more. Some of my club brothers developed hepatitis. Hard to know if it was dirty tattoo parlors or sexual transmission, but I have a feeling it was the latter on more than one occasion.

One day I decided to get EARLS tattooed across my chest. I was so proud of what I had done. I couldn't wait to show the guys my new tattoo as a sign of my undying loyalty to the club. I was crestfallen when my club brothers were upset that EARLS was not all capitalized like it was supposed to be. My lesson was learned and in a couple of days no one cared about it anyway.

I decided one day that being the only kid with a car was unacceptable. I knew of a program the DMV had where they would come to my house and teach me how to drive with hand controls. I signed up, excited to be able to get out on my own finally. I rallied my discipline enough to stay the course and get my license. I felt like I won a prize. I could drive myself around any time I wanted to instead of waiting for people to pick me up and take me out.

My first car was a white 1968 Chevy van with wood paneling in the back. I couldn't drive it because it was a standard, but I wanted it because I thought it was cool. My dad got a little money from insurance for my accident. He was saving it for something special that I needed and he bought me the van. We had a great time in the van until ten of us took it to a party one night. I passed out drunk at the party so the guys took my van home and smashed it up. It was totaled. There was no more van for me. I never saw my dad so mad.

My second car was a black 1969 Lincoln with suicide doors. It was the coolest car I ever saw. This car could be fitted for hand controls so that meant I could drive it all on my own. This time I didn't let the guys near the steering wheel. With the suicide doors I could hop in the front seat on my own, lay my seat back and throw my chair into the passenger side. The feeling of independence was incredible. Once I had control of my own car I never wanted to go back. There would be no more being driven around for me.

But my independence meant I could be at the clubhouse whenever I wanted to be. That wasn't always I good thing for me. I was at the clubhouse more than I was home.

My staying at the clubhouse full-time was making me sick. Between bed sores, just general unwellness from drinking constantly, and not really having a good way to take care of myself, I ended up having to come home for a while so my parents could help me recover. On a couple of these occasions, some of my club brothers asked my parents to come get me. The club's love for me didn't overcome the fact that those guys were unable to meet my needs. I hated leaving them but I knew I needed to get fixed up. I wish I would have just stayed home, but once I started feeling better, I'd wind up back at the clubhouse until I got sick again.

When I would be home, I had a secret I couldn't let the guys in on. My sister Joyce was dating another LORD and my parents loved him. He was around my house all the time because of my sister, and while I knew the LORDS were the number-one enemy of the club, I had to admit I really liked the guy. He was funny and nice to me, despite being an EARL. Sometimes they'd take me with them to the movies. Since I had my chair and nowhere to sit in it in the movie theater because there was no ADA back then, he would pick me up out of the car and hold me in his arms until we could sit down. I am sure he was grateful I was so lanky and skinny.

Even though I was the third wheel on some of their dates, I was glad to feel like a regular guy going to the movies and having a good time. I jumped at the chance to go out with them when they'd ask. I just had to make sure THE EARLS didn't find out. Thankfully, they didn't. Gang life was thoroughly in my immediate and extended family. Organized crime in Sicilian families was pretty big back then. There were rumors of uncles and cousins being part of it all, I don't have any confirmations, but let's just say I wouldn't be surprised. With all that and my sister dating a gang member, no one cared. It's too bad because they really should have.

Chapter 5 - A Rose by Any Other Name

I had no idea what was in store for me when I decided to go to a carnival at Holy Cross Church in the summer of 1975. I went with my club brothers. I couldn't go on any of the rides but I wheeled around with the guys, ate fried dough, watched kids run around and laughed at guys trying to win cheap prizes for their girls. It was everything a kid loves about summer nights at a fair. Carnivals have a way of making you feel like happiness is always in reach.
    Me and the guys were all hanging around in one of the clearings when this girl walked over to me out of nowhere. She was a short, cute little brunette. She had the prettiest brown eyes framed by a short, curly afro-like hairstyle. She said her name was Sue Rose. She wanted to know what we were doing there. She saw us all wearing our club colors so she knew what we were about. She said her brother was in THE LORDS but he wasn't really a big deal in that club. We chatted about nothing, like nervous conversations go between two teenagers with a spark. She asked me if she could have my phone number so of course I gave it to her. The next day she called and asked me if she could come over my house and take me for a ride in her car. I was flattered that she wanted to some and spend some time with me.
    The first time she picked me up we just drove around aimlessly. After a while we found ourselves sitting in quiet of the park parking lot. She found a spot to park that was dark and tucked in the corner of the lot. It was then that she leaned over and I reached out kissed her with all I had. My lips flushed with fever as I rushed in for the next kiss. She

didn't know it but it wasn't really possible to do anything else. I was relieved that kissing is all she was looking for. I wasn't ready to have conversations with girls about the intimate details of my paralysis and foley catheter either.

Later, she drove me home and I practically floated in my chair to the front door. After that, Sue Rose and I were an item. I had my first official girlfriend and my days of worrying if my chair would affect my love life were over.

We spent a lot of time together but she was one of the good girls who went to school. She was in school for hairdressing. She had an idea of what she wanted to do with her life. She wasn't anything like me. She used to try all different kinds of hairstyles on me. One day she put my hair in an afro. I had that for a month or two. Most of my family and friends didn't know what to make of that one. With the big afro and goatee with jet-black hair, I certainly stood out in a crowd.

After a few nights of driving around, Sue Rose decided I should come by and meet her parents. I never met anyone's parents before. Not like an official boyfriend kind of way. I met Debbie's dad at the beach but that wasn't exactly the ideal situation. And that guy certainly wasn't happy with meeting me. I wanted to get out of it but it was no use. She wanted me to meet them. I had to agree if I wanted to keep seeing her.

Her parents were your average blue-collar workers. Sue Rose was close to her mom but her and her dad didn't get along so well. I wondered what they would be like and how they would receive me. They were the average New Britain family. They made a modest salary and had an apartment on the first floor. I tried to put on a good face when I met them but they weren't interested in me or what I was about because I was in THE EARLS. Maybe it was the chair too but they wouldn't say. Her father made it known that I wasn't going to be the one he wanted to see waiting down the aisle for his daughter's hand in marriage.

Sue Rose said she didn't care what her parents thought of me. She wanted to be my girlfriend and so she was. Sue Rose was not like all the other girls that hung out at the clubhouse. The club never had a shortage of beautiful, popular girls around. While they always talked to me, none of them ever took an interest in me. To them, I had no future and they didn't want to be with the guy pushing himself around in the chair. But not Sue Rose, she came up to me first. She was the one who asked me out and she was the one who said she wanted to be my girlfriend. I paraded her around the guys and the stuck-up girls that hung around the club like a prized pony. In a lot of ways, she was the validation that I needed. I could be attractive to someone and they could look beyond the chair and find value in me.

We dated for about a year. Things were pretty heavy. We were inseparable. I wanted to marry her. She was a good one I didn't want to get away. I would do whatever I need to keep her. I went down to the local mall with all the money I had and bought Sue Rose an eighty-dollar ring. It was a pre-engagement ring but it was something. I wanted everyone to know she was my one and only. She accepted with gladness and a promise that she'd have a proper ring when it was time. How I thought I was going to pay for that, who knows. I just knew she needed to be with me.

We moved our clubhouse out of the third floor of an apartment building when the landlord had enough of our antics and the other tenants couldn't stand the sight of us. We moved into a single-family house, happy to not be bothered by neighbors downstairs to complain about us anymore. It was a real clubhouse we could call our own. It was a real dump.

Things began to heat up with THE EARLS and THE LORDS. The clubs never got along, but this was different. Animosity had been simmering for a while and us EARLS started it. One night a few of our guys went to THE LORDS' clubhouse. They kicked in the door and stole the coveted club banner hanging on the living room wall of their clubhouse.

As if stealing their banner wasn't enough, the guys took the banner back to our clubhouse where the rest of the guys took great enjoyment in burning their banner and then mailing the remnants back to THE LORDS clubhouse. It was a modern-day version of taking your leather fencing gloves off, walking over to your jousting opponent and slapping them on both sides of the face. If you wanted to ensure that you had thoroughly insulted your rival gang then this was the best way to do it.

From then on both clubs were on edge. Everyone was ready to rumble at the drop of a hat. There were fights between club members off and on, but everyone at our clubhouse was wondering what would be THE LORDS' major move against us. We all thought it would probably be big but we never anticipated what was coming.

It was Christmas Eve, THE EARLS were having a big Christmas party. Everyone was going but for whatever reason I decided to go to my aunt's house for our families annual Feast of the Seven Fishes celebration that most Italian families celebrate the night before Christmas. You would have thought I'd be dying to be at the big EARLS Christmas Party, but I didn't want to go. I can't explain it. I just wanted to have a normal family Christmas Eve instead of another night of debauchery.

The party went the usual way. As the night went on, people started going home around 2 A.M. The night dwindled into the early morning hours, and our Sargent At Arms was out doing one of his nightly rounds of walking the perimeter of the house to check for signs of trouble. As he turned the corner of the house, two LORDS knocked him out cold. With no one checking the outside and the rest of the house either sleeping or passed out, THE LORDS got to work on the most sinister of plots out of revenge for their banner.

THE LORDS came into our clubhouse and poured gasoline all over the inside of the house. With the bottom floor of the house soaked in gasoline the struck the match, fleeing the house to watch their handiwork from outside. A clubhouse of eight to ten guys woke to the sound and smell of a raging fire burning in the clubhouse. Men scrambled to get dressed and get outside. Most of them had to jump from the upstairs floor as the bottom floor was totally engulfed in flames.

THE EARLS watched in horror as the entire home became overcome with fire. Sadly, one of our club members, Frankie, died in his own bedroom as he was unable to escape before smoke and fire overtook his room. Another guy, who was just visiting for the party, died when he couldn't escape the fire from a basement room he found to sleep in for the night. It was a horrific, crushing blow to us. While THE LORDS never officially claimed responsibility to the fatal fire, we knew it was them. THE LORDS were interviewed in a local newspaper about the incident where they expressed condolences for our losses, they admitted nothing. It just added insult to injury.

I got the call about the news around 7 in the morning. I got ready as fast as I could and got to the ugly scene around 8. What was left of our place was smoldering cinder and ashes.

There is no doubt in my mind if I had been at the house that night, as I always was, that I would have been casualty number three in that fire. No one would have had time to help me get outside with the chair or to be able to scoop me up and get me out the house. By the grace of God I wanted a quiet Christmas Eve. Only the hand of God could be responsible for sparing me that fate.

The incident sent us all reeling with grief and loss. We were a club less one member and no clubhouse. Some poor sod who was just there for a night of fun was now gone and their family would be waking Christmas morning to a dead family member. The funerals took place and it kindled our resolve to get even. This incident never should have happened. We had no business burning THE LORDS' banner and getting all this going in the first place, but we were in too deep now. There was no going back.

When plans for revenge started getting laid out on the table, about half of our members turned tail and left. They wanted nothing to do with dastardly plans for murderous revenge. The mettle of every member was tested when the plans were finalized. THE LORDS would meet their fate at the end of a gun. We'd go street by street looking for THE LORDS, any LORD who might have had anything to do with it. One kid met an untimely death when some of THE LORDS came by the house. He ended up going to jail for that, but back then you didn't get much time for these things like you do now.

Two guys from THE LORDS ended up getting arrested for our house fire a year later. It was cold comfort to our pain. The day of their court date, we stormed the Hartford courthouse looking to settle the score ourselves. Mayhem ensued in the courtroom and our guys were promptly arrested. The newspapers were all over the story on this one. Thankfully no one got hurt and there was no permanent damage done on either side, but the two guys didn't get much jail time due to lack of sufficient evidence. What the courts failed to do, we were ready to make good on. In the end, most of the hatred devolved into both sides succumbing to drug and alcohol addiction and no one ended up pursuing the rivalry much after that.

My health started taking a dive around that time. The guys were no help to me and my bed sores were back with a vengeance. I was in and out of hospitals trying to get better but I always went back to the same routine of sitting around drinking with the guys and not taking care of myself. It was time to do something about my health and get well. I reached out to an agency I was told could help guys like me get help. I met with a counselor who understood my plight and said I needed to go to a rehab where I could spend some time away and get better. The truth is there was a lot of rehabilitation I could have taken advantage of years ago to help me live more independently, but I ignored it all in favor of hanging with THE EARLS. Now my body was breaking down and my life was going nowhere. I needed a change.

The counselor found me a spot at Woodrow Wilson Rehab in Virginia. My heart pitted at the thought of having to leave Sue Rose for a while but what good was I to her in this condition anyway?

I told her the night I told my parents, she was surprisingly okay with it. She understood. I mean, it's not like we were breaking up or anything but I didn't know how long I'd be gone either. Of course, we promised we'd stay together. I made the news easier for us both even if neither one of us was really sure if we meant it.

The plan to get me to Virginia was decided. My dad, Sue Rose, and a couple guys would drive me down. They were my sending party for the next chapter in my life.

Chapter 6 – South for the Better

I left a week later and arrived in Virginia after an overnight stay somewhere in a small hotel I can't remember. We all pulled up to my new home for the next season of my life. It was a large campus with lots of buildings. I don't know what I expected, other than I thought it would look like all the other hospitals I had been in. This looked like a big school. The buildings were all brick with long rectangular widows. I was excited to see what would happen, but it was scary to do something new. I was going to away from home for a while. My mom's cooking would be miles away but I had to do something positive for me.

My first impressions of the rehab weren't that good. After I was checked in, I was escorted to my room. I would be sharing it with three other guys. The prospects of having to sleep in a room lined up with beds with other patients was unappealing to me but I was assured there would be no other accommodations besides this one. I reluctantly let them put my stuff down and wheeled over to my roommates to introduce myself.

There was Carl. He was kind of white hillbilly kind of a guy. He was a high quad from an accident just like me. He was a cool dude for a hayseed. The next guy was Delaney. He was a little short pudgy black dude. He had trouble walking. He was the comedian in the dorm. The last guy was Josh. He was a white Jewish kid with an afro. He had a head injury and he was a cool dresser. He had red silk pants and a black leather jacket. These were going to be my closest friends for the time I was there. I decided the dorm room would be okay if I had to share with these guys. Their welcome made my shoulders relax that all would be well from this day on.

My first full day was therapy. I had a lot of bed sores to clear up so they put me in a therapy whirlpool tub with Betadine in it. It didn't smell that good but it made my hair shiny so I didn't mind it. There would be stretching of my body so I didn't get stiff and I'd start to learn to do more with what I had left of my arms and hands.

The nurses also evaluated me that day. They flirted with me and told me how nice my eyes were and that I was too young to have to live with a foley catheter for the rest of my life. They told me I could train my bladder to be able to urinate without it. I was all ears as to how I could live without a hose sticking out of my penis for the rest of my life. The nurses told me without the foley, I could have sex. I couldn't wait to sign up for bladder training!

After a full day, I was shown the recreation hall where I met up with my roommates and got to meet the rest of the guys at the rehab. There were guys there with all kinds of injuries. Some of them had traumatic brain injuries, others were spinal cord injured like me, some others had other kinds of physical disabilities. We were quite a motley crew of guys when we were all together. I really hadn't had a chance to just hang out with guys like me in a social setting. The experience freed me to be myself without wondering what people thought of my chair for once in my life.

The recreation hall had pool tables and music. I was all for playing pool, even if I had to learn how to play with bad hands now. There as a small cafe where you could get snacks. It was relaxed and inviting. I liked being around other people. I was weird to socialize without booze and partying everywhere. I was like I didn't know it was possible to enjoy myself without a drink in my hand. Getting acclimated socially went pretty well for a gang guy like me. Getting better was going to be good for me. I just didn't know how life changing it would be.

I thought it would be okay to be there but I was missing home. I felt lost without THE EARLS and my parents. I was so used to the club life that I never learned how to be okay outside of it. The club had a way of doing things, a way of communicating. The sense of brotherhood was strong, so strong that you'd be willing to do anything for your club brothers. Now I was just some quad dude in chair with a bunch of other guys in chairs. Who was I now?

I hung around with the guys in my dorm room when I wasn't at physical therapy. I felt that if I could at least feel close to them that I would feel more grounded on where I was.

My physical therapy was an all-day experience. They really wanted us submerged in the mindset of getting better, whatever that ended up being at the end of the day. They needed my full commitment to the process. I decided that if I had to be there, I was going to get out of it whatever I could.

The days consisted of weightlifting, stretching, whirlpools baths, and wheeling around so I could get stronger and better at maneuvering my chair. It was kind of like agility training for people in wheelchairs. Moving a chair around like a pro is a lot harder than it looks!

Feeling around, wheeling for speed, wheeling for agility made me feel strong and confident. I ate up my therapy.

I also needed to work on my hand-eye coordination. I had to learn how to use my hands and arms to the best of my capabilities. I didn't have any use of my hands at all, but the occupational therapists wanted to show me how to make whatever I had look like I knew what I was doing. This was usually with eating and trying to write.

I was willing to do anything that made me independent. The idea that I could be independent and not have to rely on people to help me so much was freeing. I wanted to take care of myself and be my own man just like any other kid my age. I wanted people to see a confident kid who could take care of himself, not some hurt kid in a wheelchair they wanted to pity.

I was hitting my stride at Woodrow Wilson and I was starting to feel good. My relationships with my roommates at the dorm started to solidify and we all started letting our guard down a little. Josh even let me borrow his silk red pants sometimes.

Sue Rose came down to see me. That lifted my spirits too. She drove my Lincoln all the way down for me so I could drive it home. It was so good to see her but something about her seemed distant to me. I chalked it up to the fact that I had been away for so long, but it felt like a splinter under the fingernail when she left. I couldn't shake it.

One of the things they had a Woodrow Wilson that I wouldn't have considered before was wheelchair sports. I didn't even know that being on a sports team could be a thing for me. They had wheelchair racing, weightlifting competitions, pool, ping-pong and Olympic sports. I got interested in wheelchair racing and the shot put. The idea that I could be a bonafide athlete intrigued me.

The guy that ran it was a young white guy. He was pretty cool. His name was Mark. I told him I wanted to learn how to do those Olympics things like the guys in his program were. He was excited to have me join. I had never been part of a sports team of any kind before. This was a whole new experience for me, never mind the chair.

I wish I could tell you we had some great training program to get us prepared to compete, but the Paralympics wasn't really even a thing then. Wheelchair sports was in its infancy and I am proud I got to be a part of what has grown to become an internationally recognized competition.

We never travelled to competitions or anything. We competed against each other. It was so much fun. In those days, the only thing we had to race in was hospital wheelchairs. We didn't have those cool, sleekly designed aerodynamic chairs the professional wheelchair sports players have. We'd clumsily get through our events in those clunky chairs. What I didn't realize right away is the confidence it was building in me. I was doing something I could be proud of in competing in sports. That stuck with me. Finally I doing investing in myself and it was paying off.

I was at Woodrow Wilson Rehab for about six months. The time I had there was immeasurable. Woodrow Wilson gave me a piece of myself back that I didn't realize was lost. With a feeling of accomplishment inside me, the plans were made by the rehabilitation team to plan for my departure home. Part of me didn't want to leave. I was safe there and making good progress, but home was a place I always wanted to go back to. I just didn't want to end up back where I started again, sick and hopeless.

I made the most of the time left that I had at Woodrow Wilson, knowing that my time was winding down. I thought of my mother's cooking, Sue Rose, and THE EARLS. When I got too homesick sometimes, I'd put myself into my therapy and my Olympic sports. Now I knew home was just a couple of weeks away. It was harder to focus on things when the reality hit that home was becoming tangible again.

My parents called one day to say they'd be coming down to see me compete in the sporting events. My dad was so proud to come and see what I had been up to all these months. He never got to see any of his boys do anything like baseball or anything like that. I think it gave him a sense of pride to see his kid doing something healthy like participating in sports. My dad also let me know that my best friend Tony from THE EARLS would be coming down with them to help me drive my Lincoln back home.

The plans were now made. I had to tell the guys in my dorm that I was going home. We were all sad to be around each other for the next couple of days. Saying goodbye is like that when you are pretty sure you'll never see each other again.

Finally, the day came and my parents arrived to see me compete and collect my stuff. My dad was beaming from ear to ear with happiness to see me. He was like that, always smiling. Today, his smile had a bit of an extra stretch. The smell of my mother's perfume was a familiar comfort. I had missed them both so much.

I competed and my parents cheered from the bleachers. I never won any medals or anything, but it felt good to try. You would have thought I made it to the Olympics the way my dad was carrying on. It was the perfect high to go out on. After the games, we met up with the rehabilitation staff to talk about my progress and what I needed to do when I got home. After that, I was free to go. Mark made me promise that I would come back to the rehab to play in the sporting events next year. He told me that he'd do one big competition once a year and that I had to come back to compete. I swelled with pride to be asked to return to be on his team again. I ended up doing just that for the next five years. Shotput and wheelchair racing remained my two events at the competition.

Tony and I loaded into the car. We started for Connecticut just as sure as anything. He filled me in on the drive about everything going on with the guys. The club was still the same old EARLS. Tony was pretty well intrenched in the gang life. He didn't see life any other way. Why would he? That's all my life was before rehab too. He went on and on about the guys' antics, the parties, the girls. Nothing had changed since I was gone.

We drove straight through the day and night. The Lincoln always glided so smoothly down the road. Before we knew it, we were home. All the familiar sights and sounds I grew up around started to envelope me.

Unbeknownst to me, my parents had a surprise waiting for me when I got home. My heart almost stopped to see a ramp outside the house, waiting to welcome me into the house. I never a ramp. Everyone had to get me out of the house and carry me down the stairs. Now I could come and go when I wanted to. I hurried out of the car and into my chair to see my dad proudly standing by the ramp, beckoning me to give it a try. They had an agency called BRS make the house more accessible for me. They made a deck to make it easier to go in and out on and to sit outside. My parents even moved me into their bedroom so I'd have some privacy instead of sleeping in the den. They took my old room instead. I felt so emotional to know they did so much for me while I was gone. The house was prepared to receive me at last. I didn't have to feel so awkward in my house any more.

My mom was excited to have me at her dining table again. Plates and dishes came flying out at dinnertime. In true Italian fashion, I was well fed by all the delicious foods my mom could make me.

There is something about everyone gathering around the table to eat Mom's cooking. Hands and spoons of food are going in all directions. The smells of love and life are intoxicating. The noise of talking and laughing was a familiar comfort I missed. I sat quietly to take them all in once again. Happy, I ate all I could.

Sue Rose came by to see me when I got settled in at home. It was good to see her, to kiss her, to smell her near me. But Sue Rose didn't seem to flow effortlessly near me anymore. It was like there was something between us now. *Maybe it is that I've been gone so long.* Did she meet someone else? She offered no information and I didn't want to ask. I was happy to pretend nothing was wrong. I didn't feel like unravelling anything unpleasant and it was clear she just wanted me to be happy I was home. After a little while, the revelry died down and Sue went home. I was relieved in a way that she left on a good note and with a promise to come see my tomorrow. It quelled my uneasiness around her for the night.

I was exhausted after a long drive and celebrating my arrival home with my family. Settling into my familiar bed felt like heaven. I felt the covers comfort me as I drifted off. My thoughts swirled as I opened the door to dreamland. So much had changed since I left. Was I the same person I was then? I knew I felt so much better about me, about life. There were possibilities now that there weren't before. I was changed, I could feel it. *Can I stay this way?*

Chapter 7 - Get Ready for Round Two

The next day, I met up with the guys at the park. Everyone said they were glad to see me. They talked up all the action I missed with highlights of gang life and fights with rival club members. It was all the same stuff. I'd love to tell you that I drove away never to have anything to do with these guys again, but that didn't happen. Without missing a beat, I was right back in the soup.

There had been some trouble with other gang members. So much so that some of the guys started carrying guns instead of knives. One of them gave me a gun and told me to keep it for my own good. I knew I wasn't supposed to have anything like that, but when someone hands you a gun you take it. I'd never fired a gun before. How I could fire a gun with my hands hardly working was beyond me. There was no time for figuring it out when there is a gun foisted in your face to receive. I stuffed it underneath me and sat on it. It was the safest spot I could think of to keep it so no one would find it.

I saw Sue Rose the next week but when the uneasiness was still there, I couldn't help but ask what was going on. Reluctantly, she told me she had gone to some kid's prom with him. I flipped when I found out she did this. I thought we wanted to get married someday. The heated discussion became an argument about disrespect and making me look like a fool. She ended the argument by saying it was time for her to move on. Just like that my Sue Rose was gone along with our future plans. I wanted to be sad about it, but the guys wouldn't let me. They'd tell me not to get messed up over some broad. None of those guys were serious about anyone really. They were too busy partying to care. Sue was the first girl to notice me after the accident. At least I knew that relationships were possible in a chair. Still, it stung that she left.

A couple weeks later a bunch of the guys and I headed north for Hampton Beach in New Hampshire again. This was supposed to be the big vacation to celebrate being home. The first night, a bunch of guys and I went up to the cottage they rented to wait for the rest of them to arrive the next day. Apparently the neighbors didn't appreciate a bunch of hooligans with gang colors partying in their neighborhood. A couple of police officers showed up that night, wondering why we were there. In true cop form, they started poking around when they decided they didn't like the looks of us.

My pulse elevated when the cops decided they would take a look through my car. My gun was underneath the driver's seat. Helpless, I sat there while they rummaged. I knew they'd find it. My fears were realized when the cop held it up for the other one to see. I was busted.

I was promptly arrested for being in possession of the gun. I had to sit in my car while they towed my car to the station. It was the best way to transport me, I guess. I was placed in a jail cell for night. It was not the way I wanted to start a vacation with the guys.

The next day they brought me to some guy's house in the back of a paddy wagon. It was some little house near the beach. The doors to the wagon opened and the man stepped inside, dressed like a judge. The kangaroo court was now in session. The judge asked me for my plea. I told him I was guilty. Without any warning, he dropped the charges and exited the vehicle. That was it. The police drove me back to the cottage as the guys had already claimed my car earlier that day. All was well with me, but they kept the gun.

The guys were surrounding me with questions, they all wanted to know what happened. No one could believe that I was just let go and that my court appearance was held in the back of a paddy wagon. I was just relieved to not be in serious trouble with the law. No one bothered asking about the gun. They all knew the cops had it. I was better off without it anyway. I'd probably shoot myself trying to use it.

Once I was settled in, the vacation was ready to begin. I was determined to have a good time, despite my brush with the law. The guys were all too happy to oblige. They were there for a good time, all

40 of them. You can imagine what a beach cottage with 40 guys stuffed into it looks like. There were guys everywhere. They were sleeping on the floor, in the bathtub, on every piece of furniture, in cars, wherever they could lay their stoned heads.

During the waking hours, it was party chaos. There was beer and weed everywhere. We'd head out early in the day and stroll the boardwalk of Hampton Beach. This small beach town had an inviting line of shops, bars, and restaurants. It also had a busy arcade. We'd stroll along, taking in the sights and checking out girls in bikinis. It was hard for me to sit out on the beach in a chair so I was happier to be in the shaded areas where the shops were.

I couldn't help but reflect on how much different my life was from when I used to run away to Soundview just a few short years ago. I might have had to struggle to find a place to sleep at night, but I had the freedom to walk or run to wherever I wanted to go. Now, I had to go where I could wheel unless someone wanted to pick me up. I loved to flirt with girls at the beach at Soundview. Now, I was hanging around a bunch of drunk guys watching them all try to score.

Beer and weed consoled me when I felt left out of the party sometimes. But those are pretty lonely companions when you need a friend. The beer flowed and the smoke billowed out of the cottage, but it was all the same stuff that went on in the clubhouse. We spent two weeks bringing sand and girls in from the beach. The nights got longer, the more we stayed. After two weeks, it was time to go home as Hampton Beach had all they could stand of THE EARLS.

We piled all we could fit in the my car the morning we left. That's not the worst news on most days, unless you need to drive three hours home in a Lincoln the size of a living room, packed with smelly hungover guys. Someone sparked up a joint and we rolled into New Britain sometime later, suntanned, broke and in need of a long shower and a good meal.

From then on I was full-time right back in with THE EARLS. All the accomplishments I had and the progress I made at Woodrow Wilson rehab were long in the rearview with The EARLS and the life at the clubhouse.

Despite all the handiwork my parents put into making our home a place I could be comfortable, I moved myself back into the clubhouse.

This was the first time my parents raised a concern about what I was doing with my life. They always loved the guys, but I was in pretty tough shape when I decided to go to Woodrow Wilson and they knew what would become of me if I let myself sink that low again.

Whether it was youth, ignorance, or a companion of the two, there I was getting drunk night after night at the clubhouse again. You'd have thought I'd be sick of the parties and the booze all the time but I was more interested in staying in THE EARLS than I was being contemplating what I was doing with my life.

The fall rolled around I was a mess in the bottom floor in a room in the back of the clubhouse. Aside from some good laughs and card games with the guys, I was getting sick again and that was no picnic. Because I wasn't taking good care of myself, I started suffering from urinary tract infections. I wasn't emptying my bladder the way I should and living on a steady diet of beer wasn't helping me stay healthy.

In no time at all, the pressure sores started to appear on my hips again. It was a sorry sight to see for everyone that loved me. I came home from Virginia healthy and in a matter of months, it was like I never left.

Around Christmas the clubhouse started buzzing. The anniversary of the clubhouse fire we had at the hands of THE LORDS was at hand and the guys were nervous that trouble may start with them because of that. Guns appeared at the clubhouse with a promise to get even if anyone came around to cause trouble. This put me at a disadvantage because with me being the only one sleeping on the first floor, I had the highest likelihood of dealing with anyone that came through the door in the middle of the night and no one to help me get out.

Thankfully, Christmas went by without a peep from THE LORDS. All that planning for nothing, but it was a blessing. I roused to go to my family's house for Christmas Eve. A full belly and a good clean time was very appealing after many weeks of partying full-tilt. Christmas Eve with my family has always been my favorite way to spend Christmas. My parents ceased that time to talk me into coming home but I'd have none of it. After Christmas, it was right back to the clubhouse for more moral decline and worsening health.

My pressure sores started getting so bad that I needed help to change the bandages on them. One of my club brothers, Gene, would help me change them and keep the wounds clean. He had an added incentive to help take care of me as he had started dating my sister Joyce, so he made himself available to help me more than anyone else. I was a wreck, a shell of who I was in Virginia.

When the pressure sores, the UTIs, and the constant hangovers were more than I could stand, I finally reached out to my dad and asked him to take me home. I couldn't stay at the clubhouse if I wanted to live. The guys understood. They could barely take care of themselves, never mind a dude in a chair. My parents hurried over to the clubhouse to collect me and my things before I had a chance to change my mind.

I felt defeated. I was right back where I started. How could I wind up here when I came home so positive that I had turned over a new leaf? The new person in charge of helping my pressure sores heal would be my mother. At least I had people at home who were lucid enough to take care of me.

My condition prevented me from being able to enjoy anything. I was sick from withdrawing from booze and my sores were a weeping, draining mess. I needed constant care to keep from getting an infection that could kill me. I felt sorry for myself for being in that state, but I put myself there. No matter how hard I tried, gang life and being in a chair just were not meant to go together.

I stated home as much as I could. I wanted to be with my friends, but I feared for my own life more than I missed them. I struggled to regain my health but the damage to my body was already set in motion. On top of the sores on my hips and feet, I developed such a bad UTI that I sent me to the hospital for a couple of months.

My time in the hospital had me reevaluating things. Despite my need to be healthy and whole I wanted this gang life so badly but I couldn't live in it successfully. Does anyone really anyway? I couldn't make it work. It's hard when you know you need to make a change but the pull to keep going back to the same thing is so powerful. What was I getting out of it anyway besides more hospital stays?

The thoughts of getting on with my life and leaving THE EARLS behind and wanting to get better so I could go back to the clubhouse swirled as I resented every last minute of recovering from my UTI. Something needed to change. I just wasn't convinced I was the one who could do it. If this wasn't a good enough reason, then what was?

If I wasn't with THE EARLS anymore, what would I do? What was I good at? Could I get a job? What kind of job can a guy in a wheelchair get that is worth the money? Trying to see the possibilities of life outside the club seemed so out of focus.

Some of the guys came to visit me but I wasn't as excited to see them as I was before. They used to be the thing that cheered me up and made me want to live again, now they reminded me of what I let go when I left Woodrow Wilson. The days are so long when you are so conflicted of heart.

I was reminded of all the work I put into competing in the games at Woodrow Wilson. I didn't know anything about shot put or anything else like that before then. Heck, I didn't think I had an athletic bone in my body. But there I was doing it with my dad cheering me on at the end. Becoming something new wasn't impossible. I needed something to focus on, a new reason to be something more. What would that be?

When I got out the hospital I came home with the resolve that I would stay away from the guys as much as possible. My parents brought me home and got me reset up in my room. It had been so long since I spent any time with them, not any real quality time. I decided it would be a good opportunity to reconnect with my family, seeing as I wasn't going to be living at the clubhouse and going around with my club brothers anymore.

I knew it wouldn't be easy to just disappear from THE EARLS entirely, but I was committed to staying away from the clubhouse at least. This involved a lot of staying home on most nights. I spent a lot of that time having coffee with my parents. We'd stay up laughing and talking. It was good to see the regular people my parents were. We got close with all the time we spent talking. I grew to love and adore my parents in ways I never imagined. They did so much for me, sacrificed beyond what anyone could ask so I would be comfortable. I felt indebted to their loving care. They only saw it as doing what they needed to for their beloved son.

Our nights always ended with my parents having to pick me up out of my chair and carry me into my room to go to bed. My dad would pick up the top part of me and my mom would take my legs. It was always hard to watch my parents struggle to get me up and over to my bed. The sadness that came over my mother's face during our night ritual gripped me with compassion for her. She didn't ask for this, she didn't want this for me, but there she was picking up her own son because he couldn't walk anymore. I can't imagine what went through her mind at the time. I hasten to try.

There were nights I longed for social interaction from my peers. I wanted to get out and see people but I didn't want to wind up back at the clubhouse drunk and sick again. I had a couple of friends still that weren't in the club and I started ringing them up to see what we could do for fun. I always loved live music so a couple of them suggested we go out to a club in town to see some bands play and see if we could pick up some girls. That sounded great to me. I was all in and in no time I was in my best clothes and driving to pick up my friends and head out to Sweet Water Bar to see who we could see.

I found the club invigorating to be in. The room was dark and lit up with funky dim lights that made the room glow with a hue of adventure and mystery. The music thumped in my chest to the beat. The band took the stage and the room was off to a musical adventure of sight, sound, and girls dancing together in a rhythmic energy that wooed me into an intoxication from everything going on around me.

That night I met another girl named Debbie. She was stunning and confident. I was thrown by her attention to me. She could have any guy in the club and she picked me to talk to. I felt like I won a prize when we exchanged phone numbers at the end of the night. She came over a couple times with dinner she made for me. We never amounted to anything that looked like a relationship in the end but she was the boost I needed to feel like I could be someone outside of THE EARLS.

I kept going back to that club. It was my outlet for socialization. I could forget about things for a while and enjoy the music. I got to know a band from hanging out around there. They were called Oreo. The lead singer was dating a girl that used to go with one of THE EARLS. They took to me when they saw my colors with THE EARLS patches on my vest. The lead singer, Pablo, was nervous that my club brothers would find out and start trouble for him. With me as a friend, he felt better about things with THE EARLS. I just liked coming to hear them play on nights they were booked. We got to be good friends after a while. I'd go to other clubs to see them play too. That year was the year I proved to myself I didn't need the club to be somebody. I could be Joe all by myself, no gang necessary.

Chapter 8 – My Love, Lynn

It was just another summer day in the city in 1978. I was out riding around with a friend in my car and when we got bored, I dropped him off at his house so I could go home. That's when I saw her. A little blonde cutie rode by me on her bicycle. She had short wavy blonde hair and light angel-like skin. Her big hazel eyes gave her a childish innocence when she smiled as she casually passed by me. She slowed her bike down a bit and then turned around to head towards me again. Her bike stopped in front of my driver's side door and she smiled down at me sitting in the car.

I barely comprehended what she said as she leaned down toward my face. "Can I kiss you?" she asked, waiting for me to respond. Not really sure what would happened next, I responded with a weak "Sure." And that was it. She leaned down and planted one on my lips. I still wasn't sure if I was dreaming when she gave me her phone number. I didn't need to ask her name. I knew who she was. Her brother was in my club, but we didn't know each other. I didn't see her the way I did that humid afternoon. She was some guy's kid sister before that day. But from that day on she'd be my love, Lynn.

I didn't want to seem too desperate so I waited a day or two to call her up. I kept it short and asked if I could take her out later on that week. She was eager to say yes.

I picked her up in my giant Lincoln and we got a couple of six-packs of beer and headed out around town to see what we could do. Our drive brought us to the park. The guys usually hung around down there and this night was no different, but I wanted to get to know this cutie for myself so we cut out of the gathering with everyone hanging around the park and found a quiet place for ourselves so we could park the car and talk.

We talked about life, family, friends, you know, stuff. We covered probably everything and nothing all at the same time. I just wanted to be around her. I didn't care what we talked about. As long as she was looking at me and smiling, that would be just fine. We sat there for hours and when I could stand it no longer, I leaned in to kiss her. It was a long, sweet kiss. If it was possible, I would have felt it in my toes.

The night got late and it was time to take her home. I dropped my love off at her house around 11 P.M. with a promise to see her the next day. I saw her every day after that. We were inseparable. I never wanted to not be with her. She was so pretty and comfortable around me. She didn't have any hesitations about me or my chair. She even had a curiosity about how my body worked and what was different. Not in a weird voyeuristic way, in a way that showed me that she asked out of caring and wanting to relate to me.

She brought up the possibilities of sex. She was the only girl that ever asked me that. I stammered a little bit as I told her how my body worked when it came to sexual stimulation and what I was capable of doing. In case you don't know, sex takes a little more planning with guys in chairs and back then there was no Viagra so you had to work a little harder to get things going. But I explained it all to her and she didn't shy away or make me feel weird about it. When I realized how comfortable she was with all of this I relaxed. Not only did she like me for me, but she liked all of me, not just because I was so doggone handsome.

Most times, we'd either drive around in my car or hang out in my room. We'd talk, and kiss, and hang out. I knew in my hear that she wasn't just my girlfriend. She was my soulmate. The more Lynn hung around the less I wanted anything to do with THE EARLS. She was my focus. Just as much as I wanted to be an EARL, I now wanted to be Lynn's everything. I knew she was mine.

Three months later, we were hanging out in my room when I blurted out, "Let's get married!" I wouldn't say it was much of a proposal, but I couldn't picture my life without her in it every day for the rest of my life. I had bought her a cheap little ring at a department store a month earlier, it wasn't worth much but it was a pre-engagement ring. It had now been promoted to her engagement ring. Thankfully, she said yes, and just like that we were planning a wedding.

I told my parents the good news. I spilled with excitement. My dad was happy for me and offered his hearty congratulations. He was like that, always happy and wishing people well. My mother, on the other hand, had reservations. She was nervous about me leaving the house and being on my own with a wife. We were so young. Lynn and I were only 20 years old, still kids. I didn't have a job and Lynn worked at a camera shop. *What business did we have getting married so unprepared for life?*

My mom's reservations rang in my ears and burned in my chest, but I was determined. Lynn would be my wife and my mom would see just how happy I would be, she and I. Neither one of us, nor our families had any money at all to put towards the wedding. Some members of our families chipped in a little here and there to pay for the required things. I am from a Sicilian Catholic family so getting married outside of the church was totally out of the question as far as my parents were concerned. We set our date for marriage at St. Jerome's Church even though neither one of us were too concerned about whether our nuptials involved a priest. To my family, the wedding just wouldn't be official unless it was blessed with by the church.

Our wedding would be in September. It was two weeks after my 20th birthday.

The special day came faster than we realized it would come. It was a perfect sunny day for us. My wedding party stayed with me at my parents' house and Lynn stayed in her apartment with hers. I was so nervous but excited to start my life with my wife. We hardly knew each other. I mean, we had just met in May and here we were at the end of September walking down the aisle to spend the rest of our lives together. But I had one thing in mind, Lynn and I would be husband and wife by the end of the day. That helped me focus when the nervousness set in. Before I knew it, they were piling me into the car and off to St. Jerome's.

Pulling up to the church took my breath away. Everyone was in their best and my wedding party was putting me in my chair and escorting me up to the church. Everything looked perfect, except for that I had my letter E on the back of my chair for THE EARLS. I wonder what people must have thought about that, me rolling into the church with my colors on the back of my chair. But there I was, waiting at the altar for her. My love, Lynn.

The music started and she appeared. The backlight of the sun haloed her like an angel. I watched her walk towards me with her Uncle Guy escorting her.

Her blonde hair was swept up into a wreath of white carnations crowning her head. Her dress was a long, straight, white gown. She was perfect. She smiled sweetly at me as she came closer. At that moment, the nervousness disappeared into bliss. My wife was by my side. She sat in a chair at the altar next to me so we would be eye level with each other. It was a consideration I appreciated. She was always thinking of me in ways like that. I hardly grasped our vows as the priest walked us through them. It felt like a blur. And just like that, we were pronounced Man and Wife. Joey Paladino had a Mrs.

Our reception was quaint but fun. We couldn't afford one of those big wedding halls with all the trimmings so we settled on a local hall. It wasn't much but it was the best we could do on the budget of nothing that we had to work with. To us, the reception was more about putting on a show for the family. We did what they wanted and got through it, but it wasn't for us. We just wanted to be together, no big event required. I guess everyone got what they wanted in a sense.

Our first apartment was a real dump. It was tiny but it was all we could afford. I didn't have a job and she was working the third shift at a camera shop. I didn't like that, but that job was all we had to live on. To keep me company when Lynn was at work, I got a dog. My first dog on my own was a Doberman Pinscher named Josie Whales. He was a great dog but he was a bit much for our tenement slumlord. When they find out we had a dog like him in the apartment they threw us out. We weren't too broken up about it, neither was Josie Whales.

We found a better place that would be more comfortable for the three of us. We settled in there just fine but seeing my wife walk out the door to work all night while I hung out with the dog was wearing on my conscience. We were living on love and not much more. I needed to man up and get a job.

My first job as a husband and a man out on my own was selling maintenance agreements for Sears. The job bored me to tears, but I was at least getting to work every day and contributing to the household. The boredom was relieved quickly as after a few months of below par sales months, I was let go. Selling maintenance agreements was not the right career move for a street kid who had grander ambitions. I just didn't know what to do next.

My second job as man of the house was selling lightbulbs for an organization that helped people with disabilities. It sounded like it was just up my alley except that trying to convince people over the phone to buy cheap lightbulbs to help out a bunch of disabled people they didn't know didn't sound like a compelling sales pitch to me either. I left that job when the monotony and agreeing with the people who said no to me on the phone got to me too much for me.

I wanted to take care of Lynn, but I didn't know what to do to make it happen. When I got some money from my accident finally after five years, I decided I would put that money to some good use to start a business for myself and Lynn. It wasn't a whole lot for a settlement, but it was enough to help me fund my dream.

I thought maybe I would open up a store of some kind. I would wheel around town with my friend Boris and look around at the stores. We'd talk about what I could do every time, but the conversations didn't amount to much until one day we walked into a liquor store and Boris kiddingly asked the owner if he'd ever be interested in selling. He answered that he would and that left me with one final question for the storeowner. "How much?"

In a matter of a few weeks, East Side Liquors became Joey P.'s Liquor Locker. I was officially a business owner at 21 years of age in a chair. There were very few guys in chairs working at all in the 70s, never mind owning their own businesses. I was proud. My wife was so excited for me. I swelled with pride that my wife wanted to help me make my dream happen. We could now build a life together. We had something we could both put into to make us the family we wanted to be.

I didn't know squat about running a store, but that didn't stop me from jumping in with both wheels. My whole family was so proud that I was a business owner. My mom and dad would come in every night to see how business was going. Sometimes my grandmother would even stop in. When I started selling lottery tickets my dad would come in and run the machine for me. You could feel the smile radiate off his face as he pressed the buttons and handed customers their tickets. "That's my boy," he would say to people as he pointed over to me and smiled. I am sure he never envisioned working for me when I was laying in hospital beds angry and immobilized. I didn't see it either. It's funny how life works that way.

Lynn started working at the store with me in the daytime to help me out. She had a job working as an assistant manager at the local Caldor. It kept money coming in when I was still getting the Liquor Locker up and running well. Being able to contribute to the house was what I needed to do to feel like I was taking care of my wife. I felt like I had arrived at that destination. I just did not know how complicated running a business could be for a kid with an 8th-grade education.

When the Liquor Locker reached its first anniversary, Lynn and I decided to realize our dream of owning our first house. It was a big leap from the disgusting apartment we had when we first married. When we decided we had enough money to look, we set out finding our humble abode in the only town either one of us ever called home, New Britain.

In hindsight, maybe we should have looked elsewhere nearby and put some distance between our dreams and the people around me. I was too tempted by the guys that kept dragging me back into their sewer of a life. But New Britain was all we knew.

In a matter of a few weeks, we put a down payment on a cute two-bedroom ranch with a big backyard. It was a white house with black shutters and trim. The landscaping was immaculate. I fell in love with it immediately. It was only $49,000, which wasn't a lot back then, but it was a big investment for Lynn and me. The interest rates then for first-time homebuyers was around 12%. That is enough to make today's homebuyers choke on their mortgage documents. We were excited and we signed on every line they told us to in exchange for the keys to the front door.

We rushed to settle into our sweet little house. It had a fireplace in the living room. It was a cozy nook for snuggling and keeping the home fires burning. We spent a lot of time in front of it imaging the possibilities. I was in my own house as a disabled man in a wheelchair at 21 years of age. That was almost unheard of back then. I kind of felt like a big deal. I was so sure of the future for Lynn and me. I was accomplished, yet full of pride. Little did I know it would be a combination that would prove to be my undoing.

A couple years back, Josie Whales got hit by a car and passed away. I didn't want another dog after that. The sting of losing my furry friend too soon soured me on dogs for a while. But the big backyard sparked my interest in dog ownership again. We had a lot of room about back to keep one happy and safe this time. I set my mind on getting the best kind of dog I could think of, a German Shepherd. When I found the right one, I named him Hans.

I loved seeing Hans run around in the backyard. Being home by himself a lot made me think maybe he needed a friend. I went down to the local pound and spotted a friendly Dalmatian that went by the name Jason.

Jason was a happy dog and loyal to a fault. Instead of being happy playing with Hans in the backyard while I was at work, he would bust out of his chain-link prison and run five miles to the store to find me. No one could believe he did it until they would see him striding up the road toward the store with ears flapping and tail wagging, signaling he was excited to make his entrance.

Things were settling in. We had our dogs, our liquor store, and our dreams for the future. What else did we need?

The store was humming right along. Sales were good and we had a steady stream of liquor and lottery business. We were well established in the community between our location and being a popular supplier of keg parties. I got a delivery truck to handle all the deliveries. Joey P's Liquor Locker was a real success.

Along with our prominence in the community came the usual types of people who like to acquaint themselves with liquor store owners. I was not prepared for dealing with the kind of situations that come with it. For one, alcoholics love alcohol but hate paying for it. Since most of the drunks that came into the store were also frequently out of work due to their condition, I was asked lots of times to start keeping a tab for certain people. They would ask me to take a bottle today in exchange for paying me the next week. For lots of those guys, the next week of paying up never came. Bottles went out the door unpurchased. I did not like doing it, but part of me felt sorry for them that life had come to that. You could see the shame in their eyes when they would ask. Their pitiful state had me agreeing to bottles on credit more than I wanted to.

The next kind of person to want to align themselves with a liquor store was people who want to sell things they stole for alcohol. This type in particular annoyed me the most. We had all kinds of things wheeling in the front door in exchange for alcohol. Of course, one had to assume that the things being brought in for booze were also stolen. Why else sell them to a liquor store? I refused these propositions at first, but I fell into the same trap as the tab people. Before I knew it, my backroom was turned into a pawn shop full of odd things that people gave me to fuel their bad habits. It is the little compromises that always lead to ruin. I should have known better. I never wanted to get involved in selling things I was sure were stolen but it happened anyway. Lynn was furious with me when this started happening. All she wanted was a quiet happy store we could call our own. Instead, things started to trickle downward, diluting our dream.

Another thing that disappointed Lynn was THE EARLS coming around to hang out at the store. They would come in for the usual supplies for the clubhouse but end up hanging around the front of the store and near the cash register. This wasn't good for business as the upstanding citizens just looking for their Friday night beers didn't want to walk past a bunch of gang members in colors hanging around drinking and smoking cigarettes. She would get upset with me when they stayed too long. She did not like the element it brought to our business. I agreed with her on the inside, but my loyalty to them won out a little too often. I would try to tell them that hanging out at the store was not really a good idea and that it was a business, not a hang out but, they mostly ignored me. The way they saw it, they were bringing me business and I should not complain. I just did not like the people they brought through the door with them. There were plenty of rumors going around town that they were dealing drugs in the store. None of that was ever founded but Lynn did not like hearing about it from other people. She worried that the cops would start coming around to follow up on the chatter. Her fears were realized when police officers started coming by frequently to deal with what had become a loitering issue in front my store. They said their goal was to clear out the hang-arounds, but Lynn and I both knew they were looking to see if there was trouble.

Business was going well, so no one complained that much. We had a thing going, Lynn and me. Just us, the dogs, our house and all the alcohol we could sell to New Britain.

I decided to buy us a boat for something to do. I had some extra money so why not? We would take our boat and our camping equipment for the weekend and sleep in our van and go boating at Wolf's Den for the weekends. Our friends would often join us. We were a regular couple with regular couple friends having fun camping. Life was good.

Chapter 9 – When the Walls Come Tumbling Down

I always had a thing for betting on football. I had been doing it since before I met Lynn. It was exciting to win a few bucks on a game here and there. But for some reason, along with the stress of running a business came more betting on football. Somehow I thought I would hit big on betting if I just bet more and more. Tensions in my house would flare up when Lynn realized I was betting all the stores money in one weekend.

    I holed myself up in my bedroom every Sunday to watch every minute of every game. Lynn was forbidden from entering. I told her she was my Black Cat. I did not want anyone messing with my luck on the games. I usually made some money on the games, but never found the fortune I saw in my mind. Other times, I would lose and not pay my bookies. Bookies do not like it when you don't pay up. They'd send collectors to my house to encourage me to make good on my bets. I still would not pay them. What were they going to do anyway, break my legs? It's not like I'd even feel it, and I had no use for these frozen legs anyway. The solution to the problem in most cases was that I couldn't bet anymore. Then I would just find a new bookie. My wife grew to resent this football ritual. My attitude on game days was full on tension, stress, and frustration when games didn't go my way. I would be unreasonably happy when I won, the manic celebrations and extra jovial demeanor was off-putting to Lynn and didn't make up for the ornery jerk I was all the other times football was on. I was exhausting to live with when football season came around.

Things were going so well for Joey P.'s Liquor Locker that I decided to open up another one three years later. We found that location on the other side of town. I saw a promotion by the SBA, offering small business loans. I took them up on the offer and found myself the owner of two stores and a delivery van just for Joey P.'s. We had grown quite a party business for ourselves selling kegs so I needed a vehicle to get it all there to encourage customers to let us supply their parties over the competition. It sounded like a great idea to me. Lynn didn't really say whether or not it was a good idea. I suspect she had her reservations, but she never voiced any.

Once the second Joey P.'s was up and running, I expected it to be double the income. The sky is the limit from here, right? What I didn't count on was what it would take to run two businesses at the same time. I wish I had given more thought to the ability for the competition around the corner to try and compete with me. Also, no matter what I did, I could not be in both places at once. This posed a problem for me in dealing with slacker employees and stealing. I tried to think of ways to make up for the lagging sales with specials and promotions, but it never seemed to take off.

The first Joey P.'s became the business that floated everything else. When that started to happen, it impacted my finances. I had to think fast. With only two years in business, Joey P.'s ended up being sold to someone else with nothing to show for it. It was disappointed but had to move on.

My brother Steven and his friends were really into Stevie Ray Vaughn. It is all they listened to and talked about. I am an R-and-B guy myself, so I had never heard of Steven Ray Vaughn. My brother implored me to give a listen. His soulful, rich blues style pierced my soul and enlivened my spirit. When Steven told me he was coming around our area to play live at Lake Compounce in Bristol, CT, I wanted to go. We bought tickets and awaited the day.

We got to the venue and I was wheeling around to check it out. I saw a man standing near the back of the hall with a whole bunch of people standing in line. I came closer to see what they were all waiting for. It was backstage passes. I decided I needed to get one for myself.

I got in line and waited for my turn. I hoped he wouldn't run out before I got to him. Maybe I was just a little hopeful he would notice my chair and have pity on me and let me have one just because. But I waited my turn and there he was, the guy standing in between me and meeting Stevie Ray Vaughn, live and in-person. There wasn't much of a fight to get one, he looked down at me and handed me my pass.

When I showed my pass to my brother, he was a little upset with me and feeling left out about me not getting him one, too. I was not too sure I would get one in the first place, and I had not planned on seeking one out at all, it made him feel a little better to know that all this backstage pass stuff was more happenstance than planning. He was happy for me to go meet Stevie and told me I had to get a picture at least.

The show was stunning. His music was better live than I ever imagined. His guitar playing was flawless and his band as complimentary as any one band could be. After a couple of encores, I made my way to the magic door that would transport me to Stevie Ray Vaughn. They escorted me out to the back parking lot behind the venue. It was encircled with tour buses, semis for equipment and Stevie Ray Vaughn's trailer. I waited for a moment outside his trailer and out he came. I didn't know what to expect, really. I had never met a live celebrity before. How was I supposed to act? My anxiousness was relieved when he walked up to me and offered to shake my hand.

The first thing I noticed about him was his demeanor. He was one of the most humble men I had ever met in my life. I expected him to be so much larger than life, but to me, he left his fame on the stage. As soon as he walked off and the lights dimmed down, he was just a regular guy who had all the same aspirations about life and the pursuit of how to live a good one. I was warmed by his hospitality and humbled by his time and attention to get to know me. We only spent but I brief time together but at the end of our meeting and the snap of a picture together, his tour manager told me I was welcomed to see him anytime he came around. It was a promise I took up on as soon as he announced his next tour dates for the New England area.

Being out at that concert lit a spark in me. I liked being around live music and the buzz of people having a good time. I remembered when I started going to clubs when I was younger. I missed the mystery and the romance of being around happy people having a few drinks and a good time. I asked my brother to let me know when he was going out to a club again. I wanted to be around the atmosphere and feel inspired like I did that night at Stevie's show.

My brother Steven was happy to oblige me along with other friends in taking me out whenever they had a plan to go somewhere. The problem with my new found interest in clubs with live music is my wife was not a partier. She was not too keen on this new Joe hanging out with his friends at bars. We had our arguments about it plenty of times. She thought I was forgetting I was married and a business owner, I thought she was being a bummer and a stick in the mud.

The more I went out with my friends, the more we fought. The more we fought when I went out, the longer I would stay out with my friends. Getting in at all hours of the morning does not make for a happy wife. I have never been a big drinker, and I've never done drugs but that didn't matter to Lynn. She didn't want me out there hanging out with people and places that could get me into trouble. I thought she was being a worry-wart and encroaching on my good time. Wasn't a hardworking guy supposed to let off a little steam?

I wish I had listened to her when she tried to tell me I was going down the wrong road. We fought more and more about it. When she gave me an ultimatum on my party lifestyle, I became bitter with the proposition and told her I would do what I wanted to do. I was the man of the house after all!

Lynn always had my best interests at heart. For that, I will always love her. The fighting turned into a wedge between us. I soured with the tension in our marriage. She wouldn't relent her objections to how I wanted to live my life. I became frustrated with the war between my marriage and my quest for fun. My answer to that became mistreating her. Yelling at her, not listening, disrespecting her with my words and even some things that crossed the line into verbal abuse became the norm in my house. I was too prideful to see that my immaturity was hurting my wife.

The tension in the marriage was mounting all the more as the liquor store and a mortgage became too much to deal with financially. I couldn't make ends meet and I started getting behind on my payments to vendors. I was trying everything I could to keep the last liquor store alive. I didn't want to admit I'd bit off more than I could chew. We lost our sweet little house on Horseplain Avenue when all efforts to save ourselves financially finally gave out. It was a crushing blow to my ego and a heartbreak for my wife. Her grandfather gave us $10,000 to get on our feet somewhere else. We found a house with a rent to buy option we could afford. It was what we had to do to salvage our lives and keep a roof over our heads.

The reality of having to sell my failing liquor store loomed in the background. I knew I was going to have to make a move to get out from under the burden on my life it had become. I had such high hopes for my future and I was watching it all flush down the drain along with my marriage. I couldn't understand how we'd arrived here. When we first started out, we saw nothing but blue skies over our lives. Now it seemed that rain clouds hovered over us not matter where we went.

I chalk it up a midlife crisis. Lynn didn't know what was going on with me or how to fix it. She was a gentle soul and hurting for consolation while fighting against her caring. She finally let me have my way when she moved out of our house and into her own apartment. I had to come face to face with how I was living my life and who I was hurting in those quiet moments of sitting alone in my house. What had I done to us?

In my pain I sought consolation in my partying friends. They were all too happy to be the company for my misery. With my wife no longer objecting to my midlife crisis lifestyle, the parties started at my house. I'd roll out the welcome mat for anyone who wanted to come by to have a drink and cheer me up. They usually brought friends. I was in pain, but I was desperate to be distracted. My neighbors didn't like the newfound Joe either. Being the party house on the block doesn't usually win points with the neighbors but I didn't care. Everything I loved was gone. My reputation might as well go along with it.

I ended up leaving that house a year later. I couldn't make the payments and I didn't care either. The money that Lynn's grandfather gave us to get back on our feet ended up being a total loss. I had to settle on an apartment I could make work with my financial situation, which was dismal. I made a move to an apartment in New Britain so I could be back in town and be closer to my friends. Why I kept going back to the same old ne'er-do-wells, I don't know. Maybe I felt better being around them knowing they didn't expect too much from me. Perhaps it was because I knew they wouldn't judge me for what I had done with myself. Either way, we got along just fine when the beer flowed and the laughs started.

I found a buyer who would give me a decent price on Joey P's Liquor Locker. He was an acquaintance of mine and he had an interest in having a business for himself. He gave me a check and I gave him the keys, along with my hopes and dreams.

I told Lynn the Liquor Locker dream was over. I know she felt bad that I was so brokenhearted about it, but inside she was probably glad that part of our lives was over. Even though we weren't living together, I still needed her. We needed each other, even if we just couldn't make the marriage work being in the same house right now.

I grew up with a kid named Joe. When he got to be around 18, he started developing mental health issues. He was weird to a lot of people, but he liked to hang around me. Right around the time things went bad for me and Lynn, Joe started coming around once a week to tell me that I needed to be saved and I needed to give my life to Jesus. I didn't know what he was talking about and his pleading was annoying. Was this something real or was this just crazy Joe talking gibberish? Whenever he started in on me about Jesus, I threw him out of my house, but felt guilty for some reason that I refused him.

I was wifeless, out of work, and living in an apartment all on my own. I felt about as useless as one can get. Though I wanted to wallow in my own self-pity, I didn't have time as I needed to figure out how to earn a living. But what to do?

I knew people around town were making scratch selling weed. For me, it would be easy money and I wouldn't have to do a lot to move it, just let people know I had it to sell. Selling kept the food on the table and the landlord off my back, but I needed to make ends meet with more than I was making as a small-time weed dealer.

I had a friend who did bodywork for a living. We had an idea to buy a smashed up car, fix it up and see what we could get for it. The first one we fixed up ended up earning us a good profit. I was bitten by the bug of used car sales. We bought a few more cars and fixed them up to see what we could get for them. This ended up being a great way for me to make ends meet, but the people that lived in the apartment complex with me didn't think so. At one point, I had a few cars in the parking lot for sale and people coming by at all hours to come see what I was selling. The used car thing ended up being what I needed to feel better about my financial prospects for a while. It was working out for both me and my auto body buddy, but it wasn't what I wanted to do with my life forever. I knew I needed to think about what I was going to do with Joe and his future.

One night, I put the TV on and was intrigued by a couple of pastors who were talking on a local channel. They were talking about Jesus in a way that I never heard before. Priests in Catholic Churches didn't talk like this. I found myself drawn into what they had to say. Was this Jesus interested in someone like me? I suddenly felt guilty about selling weed. Maybe there was an opportunity to make an honest living. Selling weed and hustling used cars probably wasn't what God wanted me to do.

I decided one morning maybe I could find a job in the want ads. You never know what you can find in there. I would spend my morning pouring over the ads and seeing what a guy in a wheelchair with an 8th-grade education could do for work. Most mornings I was disappointed by what I saw. There were lots of sales jobs, and after my stints selling lightbulbs and appliance warranties, I knew that wasn't for me. One morning I found it. It was an advertisement for a disability advocate. The job listing described helping people with disabilities understand what they could do to live independently. I thought I had best qualification they could possibly look for. I called them up and told them so, and they told me to come down for an interview.

I went to their offices to see what would happen next. I was greeted by two ladies who said they were interviewing me for the position. I wheeled into the office as an unemployed used car sales man and wheeled out a disability advocate. They hired me right on the spot. I had my first promising career position.

I was excited to see what I could do for the people who needed my help. My orientation was dizzying. I pretended I knew how to use a computer for my interview but I really had no clue what to do once I was seated in front of one. Thankfully, they had mercy on my technology illiteracy. They explained exactly what I would be doing as a disability advocate for my daily tasks.

I was supposed to take calls handling complaints about ADA non-compliance from renters. They were calls like "My landlord won't put a ramp to the door" or "My landlord won't shovel the walkways so I can get out safely," stuff like that. I would take the complaints over the phone and then make an appointment to go see them and see what they were complaining about. Next, I would take the complaints to the supervisors and we would try and mediate solutions between the renter and the landlord about resolving the ADA non-compliance situation. It was rewarding to know I could help people just like me be on their own and feel empowered to manage their own lives.

I told Lynn all about what I was doing and how I was making a difference in people's lives. She gushed with pride over what I was doing. She was so proud that I was doing meaningful work that had a real career path and something of future. Hearing her words of encouragement put wind in my sails. Lynn fueled my motivation to do all that I could to make sure I excelled in my position.

I had a coworker who was a Jehovah Witness. She was trying to get me to go to her church. She wanted to tell me what was in the Bible and I confess, I didn't know much about the Bible at all, but I knew that Jehovah Witnesses were a cult. I got myself a Bible to see for myself what she was talking about and to tell her the way it was supposed to be. I would study the Bible at night and highlight passages just so I could go into work the next day and debate her about her religion. I didn't realize what an impact the words were having on me. Why was I so interested in getting my coworker to change her mind about being in a cult?

Joe wouldn't stop coming around to talk to me about Jesus so I finally agreed to go to church with him so he'd stop yammering about Jesus to me every second he got. We went to a contemporary Christian church he was going to. I'd never been to a church like that. The people were to friendly and nice. They came up to me and talked to me. I felt like they were genuine in their hospitality. It made me relax about being there. The pastor spoke and the message he had rang in my ears and pierced my heart. I wanted more of this. I told Joe I'd start going to church with him after that Sunday. What was going on with me?

Lynn and I continued to talk on the phone and saw each other often. I was sad that we weren't living together, but I was comforted to see her and talk to her. I was always my best me when she was around. I was sorry for how I treated her. But I had to prove to her that I could be a better man from here on out. I was ready for the task, even if it meant I had to be patient with her living apart from me.

With Lynn and me working on our relationship and having a job I could be proud of, I thought I could make my way back to feeling good about myself again. These were the right steps, anyway. I had to start thinking about easing up on partying with my friends if I wanted to keep what good things I had going. I was willing to make the trade. With Lynn's support it was an easy decision.

Chapter 10 - Things Are Looking Up

I worked as hard as I could as a disability advocate. I poured myself into my job and it showed. This was good as being a guy living by himself like me, getting ready for work and to the job on time was a bit of a challenge. Getting dressed when you can't stand up should be an Olympic event. Then I had to get myself into my car, which was also a bit of a process. All of this took time, but my supervisors were understanding.

After five years, I was promoted to work with a new program that we had with the State of Connecticut. There was a new state grant was in place to help disabled people languishing in nursing homes for no other reason than they were disabled. My job would be to go into the nursing homes and tell these people they could apply to find ADA compliant housing and services to help them live independently. I was fortunate that I never had to live in a nursing home and I was thrilled to help people like me get out of what looked to me like a resignation of life.

The state set up five independent living centers in CT. The purpose of these centers was to make this program a reality. It was a monumental task, but one we were invigorated to make a huge success. I dug in to my new purpose as a disability advocate. I just never saw coming what an enormous impact it would have on me.

The grant we received was based on a law allowing nursing home patients to find opportunities to live on their own. If not, it is likely we would never have been let in the front door. Since this law was in place to allow patients to have their choice of living and they were prevented from keeping disability advocates like me coming in to talk to their qualifying patients, it was easy to find people to talk to. I would wheel into nursing homes to meet with the patients they would have that qualified and tell them what I could do for them. Most of the people I talked to were elated that they had an option.

Others listened to my presentation with disbelief. They seemed unable to imagine that I could get them out of the life to which they had resigned themselves. I was so glad I could help people. I was also relieved that most of them wanted to put the wheels in motion to see what we could do for them. That is what made coming to work so easy. I finally had a job where I could see I was making a difference, not selling booze to alcoholics so they could go home and destroy themselves, one drink at a time. It was my first glimpse at seeing that my experience in a chair was useful.

One guy in particular was all the proof I needed that I could be used to help someone else see they could live their life still. I was doing my job, making rounds at nursing homes when I was pointed to a guy in a chair named Horacio. He wasn't like the other people I usually talked to. He was a young Puerto Rican kid. I wondered if he'd want to talk to me but he was game to listen. Maybe it was because he had nothing else to do.

Before I started rattling off what I usually say, I asked him how he'd got hurt. He told me he was in a gang. He had been in a gang since his early teens and it was really the only life he'd known. He grew up around gangs his whole life. He lived in the projects in Philly with his mom. He never knew his dad and his mom was too busy shooting up to pay attention to Horacio and his younger siblings. With no one paying attention to him and teaching him to stay out of trouble, Horacio quickly found himself seeking solace in the guys in gangs that sold drugs in his apartment complex.

It was easy to get sucked into that life, I knew that. I listened intently as he told me how they recruited him to join them and how proud he was to make it into the gang and wear the colors. To him, the gang life was the only way out of his mother's grimy apartment and a life of upheaval and poverty. Every word resonated with me.

I listened in horror as he went to tell me that he had been shot by members of his own gang. They thought he was stealing from them and they wanted retribution. That is how he wound up in a chair. The gravity of gang life hit me like a ton of bricks. I had been part of a few hairy things with THE EARLS but none of them ever wanted to kill each other over anything. This was devastating to hear. Jose joined a gang to find camaraderie, protection, and guys who told him he was family only to wind up rejected by them all in the most horrible way imaginable. You could see the pain in his face while he told me. Just like most guys like him, he was too hardened to cry about it.

I told him my story of gang life too. He brightened up to hear that I understood where he was coming from. I could feel what he felt and see why he wanted that kind of life, too. He and I formed a bond that day. I told him I would do whatever I could to get him out of that nursing home room so he had a shot at a real life. He was too young to be waiting to die on the floor of a nursing home. He needed a chance, just like I had.

It didn't take us too long to find Horacio an apartment that met his needs. We had to find him a personal care attendant that could help him with his personal needs and light housekeeping as well. He couldn't believe he was actually on his own. He was so grateful. He couldn't stop thanking me for helping him. Me and Horacio formed a friendship for life. I would check on him to see how he was doing in his new surroundings and he started calling me The Godfather. He said I saved his life. I say he gave me a new lease on mine. I was motivated to do for every other young man like him what I did for him. Unfortunately, there would be plenty of opportunities to do that in the near future.

The next guy I met like him was Miguel. He was just like Horacio. Another casualty of gang life. He wasn't in the same gang as Horacio, but his story seemed eerily similar. He wasn't in a nursing home. He came into my office looking for help to find a place to live. He and I connected right away. I asked him how he got hurt and he told me how he'd also grown up around gangs and drugs in projects his whole life. He got into a gang because he had no father figure in his life looking out for him. What a job gangs do on young kids just looking for some grounding and guidance in life. Miguel was also shot by members of his own gang over a rumor that wasn't even true. How do you learn to trust when the people who said they'd never turn on you are the ones behind the trigger that puts you in a chair? Miguel was a harder nut to crack, but I was determined to reach him like I did Horacio. I told

Miguel about my gang life, too. A friendship was forged over spinal cord injury and time spent in a gang.

I was always so embarrassed by my involvement in gang. Once I was doing something productive with my life, I never wanted to look back on it. When I was a kid, being in THE EARLS was everything, now it was something I wanted to erase from my life. I could see how powerful my past was in helping young guys like me find a new chapter in life. I couldn't deny that this experience was useful. Horacio and Miguel were desperate to find someone to understand and not judge them. I suppose I was looking for the same thing.

As I went along with my mission to get people like me out of nursing homes, I continued to meet interesting people with amazing stories. The reasons why they ended up in a chair were all different, yet equally inspirational stories of survival. When someone winds up in a chair, the tendency is to think life is over and you are just going to exist until you die. I never went to those places. That served me well in life and I wanted other people to know they could go on in life, too.

I'd come home and call Lynn and tell her what was happening with the agency and the people I was helping. She was so excited for me and happy that I was feeling a greater sense of purpose. I loved to talking to her about all the good stuff I had going in my life. I was always better when I talked to her. We were seeing each other when we could. I'd pick her up at her apartment and take her over to mine. Sometimes she'd spend the weekend with me. It wasn't perfect, I wanted her back with me. We were getting along and there was no more fighting so I was happy to have as much of her as I could.

I was doing great. My finances were finally back on track after many years of being sketchy. An opportunity presented itself when my dad's landlord told him the three family he was living in was going up for sale. He told me him and my mom were nervous that the new landlord might raise the rent. I asked him what he thought about cosigning to help me buy the house. With me buying the house, he wouldn't have to worry about rent and I could rent out the third floor to someone else. That way, I would live on the first floor and make the apartment accessible for me. I couldn't think of a downside if he'd agree to go along.

We agreed to do it. I put up the money for the down payment on the house and he'd cosign for the loan. My credit was much better than it was when I had to go through the foreclosure, but I wasn't making a ton of money so I needed my dad's income on paper to make sure I'd qualify. We got the house and my parents were overjoyed that I was going to be living downstairs and there was no new landlord to worry about.

I liked living downstairs. My mom always made sure I was well fed and both my mom and dad liked to visit. They always took a nightly trip out to play the daily numbers and stop by the donut shop. Sometimes they'd take home donuts and coffee. My dad always said, "I got coffee and." That meant he had donuts he wanted me to have one.

My parents always liked my friends. Whenever I had people over, my dad would always come downstairs to say hello. He was never one to miss an opportunity to be social. When my dad was around he was the life the of the party. All the guys loved Sal. Who could blame them?

Sometimes we would have poker games and my dad got to work cracking jokes and playing bartender for us. He just like hanging out and feeling like one of the guys. I thought was nice that he wanted to help me entertain my friends. My mom wasn't much of a party person. She'd stay upstairs away from the commotion. Content to have her husband distracted for a couple hours by some guy time.

Even though I wasn't making too much money at the agency, I managed to keep selling a used car or two to make ends meet and put some extra cash in my wallet. I had my own place again and Lynn was proud of me for getting my life settled. She still wanted to stay in her own apartment. She said we were better off that way. Even though it made me sad that I still couldn't sway her to come live with me again, I was happy she was still committed to be my wife. With me settled into my new place, I saw her more often. That made me feel better.

One of the perks of working at a state agency is getting invited to fundraising events on behalf of the agency. One day we were told we were invited to a gala event for a major donor. Even the governor was invited to this one. I had never been to a gala before. The fanciest party I ever went to was a prom. We were told it would be black tie so that meant I needed to wear a tuxedo. This was a big deal and we needed to be on our best behavior. I couldn't wait to see what happens at a gala. The guest of honor would be none other than Christopher Reeve!

The night came and I got into the best tuxedo I could rent and made sure I looked sharp. I showed up to a large ballroom full of people walking around in ballgowns and tuxes, all holding drinks and greeting each other. My mind swirled with so many people and the elegance of the table settings and large, shiny chandeliers on the ceiling. It was a beautiful night, I enjoyed talking to people and telling them what I did. While most of the people were interesting, there was only one person on my mind to introduce myself to: Superman himself. Whenever I got free of conversation, I'd take a spin around the room and see if I could catch him. I hovered around him and wheeled back and forth until I finally saw he wasn't talking to anyone, then I went in for the kill. I was promptly greeted by his very large bodyguard as I got closer, but told him I just wanted to say hello. What was I going to do to Christopher Reeve anyway?

Christopher motioned for me to come over. Meeting him is still one of the highlights of my life. While our conversation was brief, it was focused. I told him what I did for people like him and me. He told me to keep doing what I was doing. Someone snapped a picture and I was ushered away. I still hold him as one of the greats. He was a brave man who endured his injury well. Many great strides were made in my community because of him. For that, I will always be grateful.

I told Lynn what happened the next day. She was thrilled for me. I wished she could have come with me. She would have looked so beautiful all dressed up. My love, Lynn. No matter what we went through. I still wanted her by my side.

Things were going great. I was happy doing what I was doing and the state was happy with our progress. I was honored to serve the people I helped for 12 years. But like most things, changes are bound to happen. The women that hired me over time moved on to other pastures. With turnover comes new personalities to deal with. That became evident to me when a new boss showed up in my office one day.

The way things ran with the previous bosses changed immediately. My new boss had a different philosophy on what constituted good work and progress. I was frustrated that the way I did things before was now being scrutinized at every turn. I never had to deal with a difficult boss before. I always worked for myself. My old bosses were so thrilled that someone like me was an advocate in this program that they never challenged anything. This boss was a different story. I didn't know how to deal with this new change in my workplace. I found my happiness and accomplishment being replaced by frustration and not wanting to be in the office. It made me sad that I was starting to not enjoy the work anymore.

People like me need a lot of supplies that other people don't need to survive, namely things to help you urinate. Some of us use foley catheters, which is a fixed tube in place that drains into a bag underneath their chair. For me, I use intermittent catheters. Intermittent catheters were a godsend to people like me who are dependent on medical supplies to help them do the normal everyday things that walking people never give a second thought.

Every month, like clockwork a fresh box of supplies would show up at my door for me to use. I needed these things. Without them, I was at risk of having a stroke and dying.

The trouble with most medical supply companies, is that they are usually really great at recruiting patients to use their services and terrible about providing good customer service to keep them. My catheter supply company was no different. Sometimes my supplies would show up on time, other times they wouldn't show up at all and I'd have to spend an hour on the phone trying to figure out where my order was. Other times, my order would be wrong and I'd wind up back on the phone again to find out how I could get what I needed in the right quantities.

The constant stress over whether or not I was going to get what I needed wore on me every month. I could have gone to another company but it was always the same thing every time. These companies were too big to care and didn't have any idea who you were anyway. You were a number on a screen and a dollar sign in their bank accounts. That's it.

The constant strain had me cursing my catheter supply conundrum for days on end. These companies didn't make the supplies, they just sold them. In my frustration on one particular day, I asked myself a question: *Couldn't I be a middle man just like them and get my own supplies?*

I thought I might be on to something. How hard would it be to be my own medical supply distributor?

I was pondering my possibilities as a direct catheter supplier, but I was distracted by being worried about my dad. My siblings and I started noticing that he rubbed his stomach all the time. We'd ask him why he was doing that but he would always wave us off. Turns out he was having pain. He finally went to the doctor and after some investigation it was discovered he had pancreatic cancer. The prognosis for people with pancreatic cancer is grim. The family was sent reeling from the news. How much time did we have with him?

My mother was a sad soul. She'd been with my dad since she was a teen. Her whole life was my dad. What would she do without him? We didn't want to consider the possibilities. What did this mean for the rest of us.

I could hardly stand to think about what life would be like without him. He was my best friend. He was my biggest cheerleader. There was nothing I did that my dad wasn't always enthusiastically encouraging me. How would I go on without him? I loved to make him proud and he'd always bragged about my accomplishments.

Then as the days went on, we were told there was nothing that could be done for him. We would just have to prepare for the inevitable. I wanted to savor every day.

I remembered going crabbing with him as a kid. We would catch crabs with chicken and go home and bring them to my mom to cook. We sometimes we went clamming at the beach, too. The beach was where me and my dad connected when I was young. I think that is why I am always comforted by the rushing waves and the smell of salt air. It reminds me of the love of my dad and sweet times with him as father and son.

In these moments of trying to get my mind around his diagnosis, I spent a lot of time reminiscing about the good times I had with him. He was such a character. There was never a time he wasn't up for a good conversation. He smiled all the time and loved to have a good laugh. I didn't want to think about missing that.

My dad always enjoyed football. Sometimes I would take him to a Patriots game. One time we went to a game in Foxboro. We rented a limousine and took my friend Charlie and my dad's friend Al. We were all sitting in our seats in the stands waiting for the game to start when I asked my friend Charlie to take me to get a beer. He wheeled me to the beer stand when I saw the band lining up to go onto the field near where we were standing. I got a grand idea. I told Charlie to wheel me up behind the band. When they started marching, so did we. We went through the tunnel and on to the field. The band went left and I went right, and straight over to the Raiders bench.

I wheeled right over to Howie Long and introduced myself. When the security came over to escort me off the field, Howie told them to leave me alone. The rest, as they say, is history. I met the entire team and got everyone's autograph and they gave me the game ball. Someone told the *Boston Herald* what happened and they interviewed me after the game. I made the paper with the game ball cradled in my arms.

Howie told me to ask for him whenever I came to a game. Of course, I did. The Raiders were my favorite team. All I had to do was tell the guy at the door I was Howie's friend and they usually let me in. It was like a dream to hang out in the locker room with my favorite football team. All because I had the guts to see what I could get away with. I think if I was any regular walking guy they would have kicked me right out. Sometimes the chair has its privileges and I use them whenever I can.

I went back to my seat finally and told my dad and his friend what happened. He just couldn't believe it. He laughed when he thought of what I had to do to make that all happen. I wished it was him who took me to get a beer. He would have loved to meet everyone.

I enjoyed a good friendship with Howie for some years. He is a phenomenal guy. I don't know what made him take pity on me and not get me kicked out of the game, but I will always be grateful that he let me hang around.

Chapter 11 – There Is No Going Back Now

As things were getting worse for my dad physically, the heat was turning up at work. The new boss that I had made it known that she did not like me coming in late or missing days off from work. No one had ever raised an eyebrow there before about my chronic tardiness. After all, it wasn't because I was unmotivated to come to work. It just took me a really long time to get ready and get into my car. But she had no compassion on me.

I was missing days because my dad was declining rapidly. Pancreatic cancer moves quickly. It was not long after the diagnosis that it became obvious that he was sick. He was in pain from the cancer eroding his pancreas. I wanted to spend as much time as I could for as long as I had with him. My mother was suffering terrible depression over her impending widowhood. It was crushing to see her so sad. My family needed me and I knew it wouldn't be long. I was scared to lose my dad. Him being in my life was all I ever knew. He supported me when no one would. For that, I was always grateful. Now, he was the weak one in need of support and I wanted to be there.

It was a particularly rough morning getting to work one day. I was running late as usual and my dad was doing terrible. My new boss took it upon herself to launch into me regarding what she thought of me being late again. That was the last straw. I told her what she could do with her job and wheeled out of there for the last time. I knew that meant I was leaving the job I loved so much, but I loved my family more. My bosses lack of compassion was just too much.

I felt liberated leaving. I was relieved to be free of the new regime at the office that had taken over what was once a peaceful and relaxed place to work. But I worried about what I was going to do for work as the reality of what I did settled in.

I didn't have too much time for wallowing. My father's final days were upon him. He was starting to get sicker and the family became more aware that we needed to spend time with him as much as we could. We decided to have weekly Sunday dinners so we could gather around the table and enjoy our time together. We all loved my mom's cooking. Italian dinners are always plentiful and loud. Just like we liked it.

When it became evident that my dad's deterioration was getting to be a lot for my mother, my sisters decided to share the Sunday dinner cooking to give her a break. It brought my dad so much joy to have his kids and his grandkids gathered around the table. Lynn came as much as she could. Even though she wasn't living with me, she was still the love of my life and a member of my family.

Lynn helped with me with the dark days of processing my dad's diagnosis. I needed to know she was in this with me. She showed up for me, just like she always did. Even on the worst days, she was what cheered me up.

As much as I could, I would take my dad down to the shoreline. We'd talk on the drive. Conversation always came easy for him. It made the ride more enjoyable. I tend to be quiet, but that didn't stop my dad from talking. He'd prattle on and I'd listen. I knew there would be a time when I would long to hear him talk to me while I drove. We'd find one of the many local fried seafood places he liked and help ourselves to fried clams and French fries. He was always looking for an excuse for getting out of the house. It probably got his mind off being sick. It was better than seeing his wife sad about his condition. I couldn't blame him for that. With me, he wasn't his cancer diagnosis. I made sure of it when he was with me.

There were days when he was tired and a little emotionally worn out from everything. It was those days when he would come downstairs to my apartment and lay on my couch. It was quiet at my place and I wouldn't bug him for anything. He enjoyed the peace and I welcomed the company.

As the days wore on, Dad got a little slower. It was hard to see him get sicker. He wasn't himself. There was a part of me that just wanted him to get better. I wanted the doctors to tell us that there was something they could do after all. I hoped there would be a medical breakthrough that some new treatment that would cure him. But we still went on, putting one foot in front of the other, marching toward the last day. It is agonizing drudgery watching a loved one go through terminal cancer. He didn't want to talk about the end game and I didn't want to bring it up. I just wanted him to enjoy his last days. If that meant he took long naps on my couch during the day, I was going to let him have it.

What do you say to a dying man? I was his son. Dads are supposed to be the superheroes. My dad was fading. It is a strange thing to be in a situation as a child and feel like you need to care for and protect your parent. I was helpless to do anything other than be there as much as I could.

My dad passed at home in his bed, just like he wanted. His children and his wife were all there to usher him to the door of Heaven. It was one of the most heartbreaking experiences of my life. Unless you have had the experience, losing a parent is a grief that can't be described, especially when they are also your best friend.

We wanted our dad to have the best sendoff we could think of. What else can you do for the guy who always loved a good party? We had a singer come in and sing "Ave Maria." There wasn't a dry eye in the house. Sal's life was celebrated for the stunning man he was. But sooner or later, the sadness comes in. Friends and extended family go back to their lives and still you are left as a family to pick up the pieces and move on. My mom, grief struck, was the hardest part of all. What would she do without her Sal? Her whole life was caring for him and making a home for his family.

I had a beautiful portrait of him painted from a picture that I always loved. He was dressed up in a tuxedo with a beautiful white carnation in his lapel, and a big smile on his face. It was his youngest daughter's wedding. The joy radiated off of his face in the picture and I was thrilled it translated onto the canvas. It came out perfect. I wished he had a chance to see it. I was comforted by seeing his beaming face on the wall as I went by. In some ways, it felt like he was still in my house. But the emptiness in my heart told a different story. Me and my mom would have to figure out how to do life without my dad. I was never so glad that I bought the house we lived in. At least Mom had me downstairs when being home alone got too much for her.

Ever the housekeeper, my mom cleaned my house and make me food to get her mind off of the grief. It was good to have her around, even if she made me crazy sometimes. She flourished when she was caring for someone. I let her make me her new project.

Things settled down after a while and my mind got back on what do with the next chapter in my career. I picked up my interest in seeing if I could be my own medical supply distributor as the issues I had with my current supplier weren't any better and I was itching to find something to do to take the place of the aching loss I had over losing my dad. I had no idea how I was going to make it all happen, but I was going to see what I could do anyway. Why not?

I started by calling the state insurance agencies and asking them what I'd need to have so I could bill them. They told me I needed a license to sell medical supplies in the state of Connecticut and told me who to call. My new project would be getting my license from the state. Much to my dismay, it wouldn't be happening overnight. There was a pile of paperwork to fill out and I had connections to make. In short, I needed something to sell if I wanted to be licensed to be a medical supplier.

While I was working on my medical supply project, I was going to need to bring in some money. I had me and my mom to think about when it came to making the mortgage and selling a used car here and there doesn't exactly make ends meet. I had some unemployment coming in from leaving the state agency, but it was hardly enough. I was going to have to find my next gig. I found an ad for a position helping kids in an after school program and applied.

I didn't have much experience with kids aside from my nieces and nephews, but they didn't seem to mind. I was dealing with babysitting a whole bunch of kids for not much money. I agreed to do it and they agreed to hire me. I didn't have to do much, just keep everyone safe and alive. I had to make them mind, which usually meant distracting them with games and stuff to keep them occupied until their parents picked them up. It was noisy and chaotic. I wasn't used to a swarm of kids buzzing around me. It took some getting used to, but those kids wore me down after a while. I started caring about them. I wanted to know where they were from and what they wanted to be when they grew up. Kids perk up real fast when someone takes an interest in them. We started to make some friendships happen and it made the afternoons more enjoyable. I spent the school year with them. I was sad to see them go. While I missed them, my summer days were a whole lot quieter. It's funny what you get used to. I just hoped some of those boys wouldn't end up going down the same dead end road I did.

I was enjoying my time off but if I was honest, I could have done with a little bit of a social life to get my mind off my dad and the fact that I didn't have much in the way of a job right now. A friend of mine from the state agency I worked for, also a wheeled warrior, called me up to ask me if I'd be interested in coming to a wheelchair rugby game with him. He had been playing for a while and wondered if I'd be interested in checking it out. Aside from the Paralympic events at the rehab I did when I was younger, the last thing I did was play sports. Still, I was at least interested in seeing how a bunch of guys in chairs played rugby. I mean, wasn't rugby a full-contact sport?

I met Rick there and he introduced me to the guys. They all got out of their regular chairs and into special wheelchair rugby chairs. They were strapped in and even duct taped into place. My mind raced with why someone needed to be taped to their chair. I found a spot to park and prepared my mind for what this game would be like.

The refs got the game started and off every one went in the quest for the ball. Chairs were darting everywhere and I cringed with the sound of smashing metal ricocheting off the walls as players rammed into each other, sometimes sending players spilling onto the floor. Team attendants would scoop up the fallen players and get them back into place, sending them off to do it all over again. It was brutal. And I had to learn how to play. It was the kind of aggression I was looking for to take the edge off the stress.

As soon as the game was over Rick asked me if I'd be interested in playing. I could hardly wait to say yes. I went home excited to start my new hobby, and waited for practice day so I could officially be a wheelchair rugby player.

I told Lynn what I had decided to do. She thought I was crazy. Who would want to barrel into someone in a wheelchair to get a ball? The thought of it was exhilarating. She calmed when she realized how set I was on playing. I guess she was used to me doing screwball things by now. I told her I hoped she'd come to our games.

My first practice consisted of warmups like wheeling in and out of cones and racing back and forth across the court. I had to learn how to build up speed and how to be more agile with my movements. I was fun to see what I had in me. I had done racing at the rehab games so I knew how to get going. It was easier with a wheelchair rugby chair instead of the hospital chairs we used to race in at the rehab. These special chairs were built for speed and sudden movements. The wheels were pitched out to be more stable and capable of taking a hit.

Then we played. I had a blast. Playing wheelchair rugby made me feel free and strong. It gave me more purpose and camaraderie with the other players. I was hooked.

The new involvement in wheelchair rugby gave me the boost I needed. I was invigorated to keep doing what I needed to build my new medical supply business. Making this thing happen was going to take stamina and a desire to press forward. In some way, I needed wheelchair rugby to remind me of the importance of tenacity. I already had the hustle. I just needed to determination to make it happen, no matter how long it took to make it happen.

I plodded along with my paperwork, stipulations, qualifications, and certifications with the state to get my license for what was now going to be my new medical supply business. What does a guy with an 8th-grade education know about starting a medical supply business? Knowing nothing about the industry didn't deter me from getting into it one bit. If life in a chair taught me nothing else, it taught me to grit my teeth and figure things out for myself. It is amazing what I was capable when I put my mind to it. This would be no different as far as I could tell.

The next hurdle was to figure out what I needed to do so I could bill insurance companies. Medicaid and Medicare requirements were the biggest contracts to get and they had the most to lose. I didn't know what I was doing, but I kept doing whatever they told me to. Sure, I felt in over my head. But what else was I going to do with my time anyway? Trying to deal with the grief of losing my dad was almost unbearable, seeing my mom so heartbroken was devastating to watch. Working on getting this business going was the respite I needed from all the emotion swirling around the house.

I spent a lot of time on the phone with state agencies, the Medicaid office and anyone else who could tell me what I needed to do to be a bonafide medical supply business. I started to think about what I would do once I got there. What would I sell? Was this going to be something I could live on? It's funny how when you are in the middle of something you wonder about the possibilities. But I didn't get too hung up on dreaming. I had already failed at one business, I didn't want to be disappointed again. I just kept my head down and focused on all this dizzying paperwork and waiting for approvals.

After about a year and a half, I finally made it happen. I couldn't believe the state let me be a medical supply company. Finally, New Britain Medical Supplies was officially born. What was I going to do now? I wanted to go big. I wanted to sell anything I could to someone like me. I set my sights on selling wheelchairs, medical beds, hygiene equipment, anything a person in a chair could need. I wanted to be the one stop shop for all things for the wheeled life. Of course, we would sell catheters. That is the reason I got into this in the first place. I wanted to find a way to make getting my urology supplies a lot less of a headache. I thought other people like me would want that as well.

My next logical step was to get customers to buy from me. My wheelchair rugby team were my first targets for business. It was an easy sell. They buy from me and I make their life easier by not having to worry about getting supplies on time and without issues. Besides, they knew me. At all the other places they were getting their stuff they were a number to a faceless voice one the other end of a sea of customer service agents. It was a no-brainer for them. My first success with New Britain Medical Supplies started with five patients who were my friends. I was off and running. I was great at thinking big and having the drive to make things happen, but figuring out how to bill insurance companies was another thing. Insurance companies have their own system for billing submissions and you have to know exactly what they are looking for in order to get them to pay you for what you sold to your customer. I had a lot of learn in the insurance space.

I got a computer and some pens and notepads. I was ready to rock. Starting a company in your living room isn't very exciting. There is no ribbon cutting, no big sign on an office door. Just you and your dreams, and for me, five friends who promised to be customers as soon as I was all set.

The state of Connecticut came over to help me set up all the billing system stuff they had so I could bill Medicaid. It was such a relief to have someone help me get my act together so I could bill Medicaid properly.

I was just starting out and I needed space to work and store stuff so the only viable option was the start New Britain Medical Supplies would be in my living room. I wasn't too concerned about it. After all, most great companies were started in someone's garage. I would be no different.

Lynn was so proud of me, despite the humble beginnings. She was always proud of me. That's what I loved about her. She always wanted me to do well, even when she had no idea what I was up to. Like this time. That made two of us. I wasn't sure what I was up to either.

Since I couldn't pay anyone to help me, I had to hit the streets and find some new clients. I made appointments at all the local Urology offices I could find. I'd go see anyone who would agree to let me talk to them. I went to all the rehabs to tell them what I was doing. I thought being in a chair may give me an edge with them. If I could sit with someone who could refer a new customer to me on any given day I was happy.

I got a new van I could drive and put my logo on it. I wanted everyone to know I was in business. Things felt hopeful.

Lynn started getting sick a lot. She was a smoker so she always had that typical cough but she was getting little bouts of pneumonia and having breathing problems out of nowhere. We dealt with that for a while, but it was clear something more should be looked into.

We made appointments to have the doctor do more digging into Lynn's mysterious recurring pneumonia. The doctor did a chest x-ray and found something on the film. Her next step was to do a cat scan to get a better picture of what the radiologist saw. We sat in the doctor's office for the news. Lynn had lung cancer. My heart sank. I felt so badly for her. What did all this mean?

Lynn was referred to an oncologist for treatment options. Chemotherapy and radiation would be the treatment she needed to get better. The treatments were grueling. It was hard to see her go through them. Still, I was there for here. Her battle spanned two years with plenty of complications. She developed fluid around her heart as a side-effect of all the treatments she was doing. It was hard for her to keep weight on. I was helpless to do anything to stop the progression, despite taking her to Dana Farber Cancer Institute in Boston to see if there was any more they could do. The inevitable was sure to happen. There is no way you can brace yourself for that. No matter how much you go over what the details will be like in your mind, you can't prepare yourself for the pain. When she got too sick to be on her own, she moved back home with me.

My love, Lynn, transitioned from this life at my home in her bed on a Fall day in September. I could hardly stand to think about what life would be like from this day forward. Time moves so slow when you are overrun with grief. I threw myself in to my business to try and drown out the pain. No matter how hard you work, there is no way to avoid it. I was crushed. My wife, my one and only, the love of my life was gone. I didn't know who I was without her.

Chapter 12 - Keeping the Train Rolling

I had my niece, Chelsea, come over after school to help me keep my paperwork organized and help me with gathering all the information like insurance information and prescriptions from doctors I needed to bill Medicaid for my customers.

I was starting off on the right wheel. I just had to keep this medical supply business rolling in the right direction.

My business grew steadily. There were lots of bumps in the road. I was learning as I was going. One of the biggest mistakes I made in starting New Britain Medical Supplies was trying to be a one-stop shop for all things medical supply. I thought thinking big and carrying everything would help me make more money and earn more customers. It ended up being more of a headache than I planned on.

First of all, I had to find a lot of space to have things in stock. I had two garage bays out in the back of my house, but they filled up quickly with medical equipment and before I knew it we were wall-to-wall with things hanging around for sale to anyone who asked for them.

I did that way longer than I should have. I had my brother and my friends running all around Connecticut setting up hospital beds and delivering things. I wished I had more to show for all that work than I did. But I kept trying.

As things continued to grow, I had to find more help to keep me going. I needed someone to help with all the paperwork and office stuff. I was not very good at keeping things organized, and if I am honest about it, I didn't particularly want to do it either. I put an ad in the paper to find an office worker. I had some fits and starts with people, but I kept looking for the right one. My niece said her friend's mom was looking for a job. She was a friendly, professional lady who knew a lot about computers. I didn't know anything about computers so I thought she would be good to have her with me.

This woman ended up being exactly what I needed to get things to the next level with my company. Up until then, I was only taking state Medicaid as an insurance. It was good income, but I needed other insurance contracts to grow my business the way I wanted to. In short, I didn't like telling people I couldn't take them on as a customer because I couldn't take their insurance.

Hartford, CT, is the insurance capital of the world. All of the insurance companies that I wanted to talk to were right in my area. I called on everyone I could think of. Trouble was, they wouldn't take my calls. Even when I got through to someone on the other end of the phone, I got pat answers that they were not looking for vendors and told, "Good luck." When I had my fill of patronizing calls from faceless people in skyscraper offices, I made a decision to go in person to pay them a visit. I wanted them to see who they were turning away.

Much to my delight, almost everyone one of those insurance companies finally said yes to approving me as a vendor once I visited them. I guess it is hard to turn away a guy in a wheelchair, so score one for the Quad Team. With all the new insurance contracts came a lot more business. My niece, my office manager, and I needed a lot more manpower and space than we had. The living room and kitchen in my home just weren't cutting. We were finally in search of office space.

I pained over the fact that Lynn couldn't be there to see all that was happening in my life. She deserved to enjoy the spoils of my labor. But she would have to watch what was happening from above. I felt accomplished that I was making something of myself. I wished she could be by my side while I did it. There was so much that I wanted to do for her, but I never had the money to do it. We never took a big vacation, I never bought her a fancy new car. I would have loved to be the guy to do that for her, but it wasn't meant to be. I liked to think that she knew that my plans, even though she never said a word about it.

We found our dream office on the top floor of a three-family turned into an office building right in New Britain. It was on a street adjacent to the Walnut Hill Park. The location was perfect and the neighborhood was serene. It was accessible for me, so I wouldn't have any problems getting into work every day. We signed the lease and made our plans to relocate. I was a legitimate business owner with an office now. The possibilities felt endless to me.

Church had become a regular thing for me and crazy Joe over five years. I couldn't wait to go on Sundays. One service the pastor announced that they would be doing baptisms in a month and to let him know if you wanted to get baptized. I went up to the pastor and told him I wanted to get baptized. This took some planning because, I had never even been to a baptism like this and I was in a chair so we had to figure out how to safely get me in and out of the water. He did a little devotional with me and we talked about what it meant to be baptized and asked me if I was ready to publicly confess my love for Jesus this way. I was. When the Sunday came, I could hardly wait.

There I was going from gang member and local hustler to washed clean by the blood of Jesus. Even I could be accepted by Him. What a feeling to know that I was not too far gone to be saved. I wished Lynn could be there to see me soaked and happy to be God's son.

I finally had to make the decision to curb my offerings to the public on what I wanted to sell. I didn't have the storage for anything else in my new office and my garage bays were packed with stuff that needed to go. My initial reason for wanting to do this was about me not getting my catheter supplies on time. I decided to scrap all the wheelchairs, and hospital beds and just focus on what people needed the most; monthly supplies.

Selling monthly urology supplies was a no-brainer. People needed them every month and they couldn't live without them, so I'd always have a customer as long as I treated them well. That was the problem I had with all of my urology suppliers before, I was a number and no one really cared. If I made these people feel like they were my family, there shouldn't be any reason they wouldn't use me. My motto for New Britain Medical Supplies was to wow them with customer service. That is what I did and that is how my business grew well beyond my expectations.

We were so good at treating customers like family that we needed to add a biller and another order taker to the team. The growth was dizzying. I never made money like this before. I loved having the freedom of working and going to Florida for a week when I wanted to get away.

While I had enjoyed my time with wheelchair rugby and playing with the guys, the business and my love of Florida kept me from participating as much as I wanted to. The guys understood and I came to see them play when I could. They'd always rib me and tell me to get in a chair and come play, but I had other interests to focus on now.

My mind was starting to change about being a widower and alone. I loved Lynn with all my heart but was I supposed to be resigned to being alone for the rest of my life? I still had a life to live, didn't I? The thought crossed my mind to consider dating again. It sounded exciting, but I was with the same woman for almost 30 years! What did I know about dating, really? I was just a punk young kid when I met my wife. Were the rules the same? What was it going to be like dating a woman my age?

If I wanted to meet people, I'd have to get out more. I was so focused on my work that I didn't consider getting out to meet someone new. It's hard being a widower. There is the space between losing someone you thought you'd always have and getting to the point of welcoming someone new that is awkward. When is it time to move on? What will people think if you do? Could I love someone the way I loved her? These are the anxiety-producing questions anyone in my situation has. Is it insulting to your dead spouse to want to be with someone else? These questions kept my mind preoccupied and clouded my decision to make myself available. Still, being out and about could only be good. I needed to feel like I was coming into the land of the living again.

Wallowing in the happy days of yesterday was starting to get old, even with the success of the business.

The first order of business was to start hanging out with my friends somewhere that I could meet new people. You can't meet someone new if you aren't in places where there are new faces. I always liked going out to see live music before. It seemed logical to start doing that again.

I started hanging out at the places where someone my age would be out listening to the kinds of music that I liked. After a few weeks, I started getting to know the band members of couple of local bands that I liked. It was fun to get to know them and to find out where they played on the weekends.

I dated a few ladies that I met from a few bars that I frequented when I went out to hear some music. They were mostly my age and we had fun dancing, but there was just no love connection. We remained friends and it was always good to say hello when I saw them out without hard feelings.

As luck would have it (or whatever you call it), through the magic of social media, I ended up friending a woman I used to work with at the agency a few years ago. We were just friends but I enjoyed talking to her and she was easy on the eyes. I thought maybe we could at least rekindle our friendship. Our text messages became a regular thing and I thought it would be okay to consider her as more than a friend. The only problem was she lived in Colorado.

She was from Connecticut originally. Her family lived a few towns over from me. She had been planning a trip to visit her folks right about the time we started talking so it was clear that a reunion of sorts for us was in order. As we continued to text and catch up on life and the happenings in between working together and moving on, we put a concrete plan in place for making our meeting an official date.

The time finally arrived for her visit. We had planned to meet up while she was in town but our date ended up with her spending two days at my house. It was thrilling to have her with me, but it had its challenges too.

She was a free-spirit kind of girl. She was one of those Whole Foods shopping, Birkenstock wearing types. She was uninhibited in almost every way. I think her approach to life was initially what attracted me to her. There was something exhilarating about being around someone who lived in the moment and cared about nearly everything around them. I admired her resolve to protect the environment and to care for all living things around them. But as someone who is not especially attuned to this way lifestyle, her philosophies started to chafe me. Being around someone like that when you don't live that way becomes inconvenient. I was willing to overlook it all at first. I put up with out of the way drives to have to get things that were 100% all-natural and biodegradable when we could just easily go to the local store for something less environmentally conscious for half the price.

When she went back home to her parents house for the rest of her trip, I was sad and relieved at the same time. I loved the company and the fact that she was completely comfortable with me and all the biological things that happen with me as a spinal cord injured man. She was nothing like anyone I had ever dated before. I am normally attracted to women who wear high heels and makeup. She was nothing like that. She wore no makeup and 100% organic clothes. She was pretty, but the natural life made her come off a certain way I found a little off-putting if I have to be honest.

She decided after her trip out that she would come visit me every couple weeks so we could keep our relationship going. I was all for that. She'd fly out for the weekend every couple of weeks to see me, but each time it became more and more apparent that she wasn't my type and I probably wasn't ever going to warm up to that.

As the months progressed, she started to press into me about sharing the traveling so we could see each other. I had no interest in getting on a plane to go to Colorado any time soon. Besides, her apartment wasn't probably going to be accessible for me and I had no idea how accessible Boulder was anyway. I don't like going to places unless I know I can get around. She bristled over my concerns. As the conversations continued, she became more defensive about my unwillingness to take a chance that I would be okay coming for a visit. The difficult conversations became fights and I didn't see a way out of it. Neither did she. I wasn't coming out and she didn't want to be the only one traveling. After about five months of this, we agreed our relationship wasn't meant to be. By the beginning of the following year, our relationship was done.

Honestly, I was relieved. It was fun to have a relationship, but when the idea of a relationship turned into reality, I didn't want to do it. I am sure that our differences in philosophies of life and geography had a lot to do with it. I just wasn't ready to completely give myself over to a relationship right now. My heart was too focused on my business.

Even though I wasn't ready for a real relationship I still liked the idea of entertaining ladies, even if we were just casually dating. I guess my single life started to bother my friends because they kept suggesting single friends and family for me to meet. There were hits and misses. Some characters right out of a funny story, and some women who just had their minds focused on other things.

I was doing well financially and that became apparent to the interested women who came around. That started to be a concern for me when they would ask me for things or ask to borrow money. That bothered me a little bit. I didn't want it to make me start to mistrust women, in general. I wanted meeting new women to be a good thing, so I got rid of the women who were looking for a free ride real quick.

I started to miss having a dog around. I loved dogs and being alone in my apartment was isolating at times. After some looking, I settled on a beautiful Brittany Spaniel puppy. I named her the best name I could think of: Babe. Babe was what I called Lynn. That was my pet name for her. It would be kind of nice to yell out, "Babe!"

She was the prettiest dog I ever owned, her soft white and rust-colored fur flowed from her ears and her legs. She was a darling, but man, was she hyper! I should have considered the amount of energy that a spaniel has and she had it times ten! As she continued to grow, her energy level and her penchant for getting into trouble grew with her. I loved that dog so much but she drove my mom to the brink of madness with her digging. Babe dug up nearly every flower my mom planted and there was little I could do to contain her. After a while, it became apparent that Babe needed a place where she could run and an owner that could spend more time training her than I could. I had to make the heartbreaking decision to give Babe to a friend who was better able to raise a spirited spaniel like Babe. I was crushed to leave her at my friend's house but I knew it was best for her. I hoped somehow she would understand as I said my goodbyes and drove away, leaving Babe in the rearview mirror of my heart.

The business continued to grow and the weight of responsibility, not to mention State and Federal regulations were weighing on me. There is so much to keep up with when you do business with government insurance. I worried about doing the right thing. The State and the Medicare were auditing our records and our bills to make sure we were billing correctly. As we grew, the audits got more frequent. Having to deal with Medicaid and Medicare audits was stressful on me and my office workers.

The way that it works is that if they find mistakes you have to pay the money back that they already paid you. That was the worst part about it. We had to make sure everything was in order so we didn't have to deal with bad audits and losing money on goods we already sold. It is in this regulation stuff that the fun of having a business can get sucked into the void. I loved wowing customers and making friends, but the day-to-day paperwork and rules stuff was not for me.

Staying with just Urology supplies paid off big time. Calling up customers to ask for their monthly orders was like ringing a cash register all day. There was no real sales pitch. You either needed catheters or you didn't. If you did, I wanted you to be my customer. If you keep your customers happy, they will always be back the next month. That is how everything came together.

Even with the antics of Babe and my broken heart, I still wanted a dog. I needed a companion who would be there with me. My younger sister had a few shih tzus and she loved them. They were cute and a lot less trouble than a spaniel so I asked her where I could get one. A few weeks later, I had a new addition. He was a grey shih tzu I named Jake.

Jake was a tiny little puppy. I was nervous that I would run over him, he was so small. He was an attentive pup who didn't make too much noise or get too crazy. He had just the personality I was looking for. We settled in as a couple of bachelors in my apartment. Jake and I were roommates and we were friends. My dog lover's heart was mended at last.

Chapter 13 - Rain Clouds Are Sure to Come

My friend Jimmy showed up at my house one night and brought up the subject of traveling with him to Florida. His family had a condo down on Cocoa Beach and he thought it would be good for me to get out and take a vacation. I told him he was crazy and that I hated flying. Since Jimmy can be a big pain, he asked again and I agreed to go. I couldn't believe I said I would. What was I going to do in Florida? I had this business. What would I do with that? I talked to my office ladies and they told me not to worry about it. Everything would be fine if I took a little vacation. I was out of excuses not to get on a plane. I was going to Cocoa Beach.

Jimmy and I got a room at the Marriott right on beach. Once we checked in, we headed out to see what was around. I couldn't get over how beautiful everything was! The flowers, the landscaping, everything was green and tropical. I couldn't stop marveling and pointing things out to Jim. I wheeled around and took in the scene. I was hooked.

The week went by too fast. I spent the next few months dreaming about returning to my magnificent Cocoa Beach. When my sister Lisa started talking to me about a hotel in Miami called the Fountain Bleu, I told her we would go. Next thing I knew, my sister Lisa, my niece Chelsea, and me were all sitting by the pool at one of the hottest hotels in Miami. It was then that I decided that the Florida lifestyle was definitely for me. I could get used to this. I wanted to find somewhere to call permanently mine in Florida.

One of the things spinal cord patients who catheterize have to deal with is routine kidney tests. I am no different. Every year I have to have to have an ultrasound done of my kidneys and this time was no different. It was always more of a pain than anything. I hate doctors and medical tests. I spent way too many days in a hospital to ever recover from that. I would just assume the whole medical field just leave me alone but being in a wheelchair does not afford me that luxury.

My urologist told me it was time and set up my appointment. As far as doctors go, I liked Dr. Stein. He was young, smart, and he shared my love of football. I ended up with him because my other Urologist retired. Me and Dr. Stein had a friendly doctor/patient relationship going, so I felt comfortable bantering with him. I usually buck tests, but this one I was fine to just get over with.

The morning of this ultrasound was the same as any other. I hated going and I had to get it out of the way so I could forget about it for the next year. As is customary, I always try to badger the ultrasound technicians into telling me if everything is okay. They almost always tell me they can't, but after lots of prodding, I can sometimes get them to say something. This one wouldn't budge. She performed her test and right after, she got up and left the room. I didn't think anything of it at the time. I thought it was weird, but nothing serious. She came back in and sent me on my way with "Your doctor will be calling you." That made me think. No one had ever said it like that before. She said it like she knew he needed to call me. It was a Friday when I had the test done. I had to think about it over and over in my mind while I waited for the doctor to call me on Monday.

Dr. Stein called me on Monday morning. I didn't hesitate or make pleasantries. It sounded like he was grateful to not have to wait to break the news either. He broke into what he had to say to keep from any awkward silence. "Now, don't freak out. We found a mass on one of your kidneys. I took out three kidneys last week, Joe." He chuckled a little to bring some levity to the news but all I heard was "Mass."

The doctor told me I'd need a biopsy done first. He told me it could be something as simple as a cyst so to not go off the deep end and plan my funeral yet. The biopsy was planned for two weeks later so I didn't have to wait too long. With any luck, it would be an easy and benign explanation. The biopsy would have to be sent to a lab so there would be no immediate news. But I knew he knew right away. The lab tests were more for me than for him. We both knew that.

The conclusive biopsy results came three weeks later. I had cancer. The news hit me like a truck. I didn't want to have cancer. My wife died of cancer. I watched what happened to her. I couldn't stand the thought of wasting away slowly as cancer claimed my body. I didn't want to endure the pain I watched Lynn go through. What would this do to my poor mother who already witnessed her husband and her daughter-in-law die of this dreaded disease?

The best possible solution to this problem was to have the kidney removed. Dr. Stein explained confidently that a removal of my left kidney was the only way to be sure that all of the cancer would be gone from my body. The doctor told me with a total kidney removal there would be no need for chemotherapy or radiation. I liked the sound of that.

I could hardly stand to wait for the day to come. I was scared about going under and I didn't want to be in a hospital, but I had to do what I had to do. I was more interested in being cancer-free than I was panicking over hospital stays. My surgery would be early in the morning, that way I wouldn't have to work myself up all day waiting. As much as I hate early rising, this was one day I wouldn't mind as much.

My younger sister picked me up to take me to the hospital. I'd have to be there for four days. There was nothing I wanted more than to have the surgery and go home, but my doctor wouldn't hear of it. I would have to deal with a hospital stay once more.

My sister waited for me to finish my surgery. I was grateful that someone was waiting for good news that I was done in the waiting room. My surgery went without complication. I was now Joe with one kidney.

The hospital stay was agonizing. I wanted to go home. I had things to do, a business to run. I didn't want to deal with nurses and hospital noise. Finally, after the fourth day I was cleared for takeoff. I was never so glad to see my apartment. Even if it was a little lonely, I had my best furry friend Jake to great me. I still had my mom upstairs who made it a point to take care of me.

My mom became a welcomed friend to me in my widowerhood. We enjoyed most meals together. She would cook and bring the food down to me and we'd both sit at my table and talk a little bit. For both of us, it was a whole lot better than eating across from the empty chair that used to be where our spouses sat. The isolation that losing a spouse can bring is hard to describe. It's like a hole in your heart suddenly finds itself on the outside of your body every day. I was glad my mom was there to ease the pain, even if she didn't know that is what she was doing for me. I knew that if anything happened, I could trust her.

I continued to feel better as the days went on. The incisions on my belly healed. You could see where the doctor make small cuts on my stomach to detach the kidney and then a larger one underneath my belly button to remove it. It looked like someone stabbed me in the gut about five times. I couldn't really feel any sharp pains or anything, just a general notion that my body wasn't happy with the trauma that surgery caused. I felt tight and had more spasms than usual. But as I healed my body calmed down, letting me know that it was fine.

The doctor told me everything looked great and he didn't see any issues. He also told me that to be sure, they'd have to do an ultrasound of my belly and do a chest x-ray every three months just to make sure that the cancer didn't pop up somewhere else. I would have go through those stupid screens a lot more often but if I wanted to make sure I was healthy, that's what I had to do.

I guess what you do after you get the *all clear* for cancer is move on with your life. That was a good thing because my business was growing so much that I didn't have time to sit around and feel sorry for myself. I had been engaging in rehabs in the area to try and get them to send me patients after they discharged. Luckily, rehabs that specialize in spinal cord injury like doing business with spinal cord injured patients. They sent me patients as long as I stayed in front of them. It was a win-win for us all.

Since I was becoming a local bigshot of sorts, I started getting involved in the Spinal Cord Association of Connecticut. It is an organization of spinal cord injured people that want to help others like them succeed. They did fundraisers to help award grants to those with spinal cord injuries. Every year they had a gala to raise money for their causes. Just like the one I went to with Christopher Reeve, this was also a dressy event. Local TV celebrities would come and emcee, they usually had a famous person in the spinal cord community come and be the keynote. It was an impressive event and as a business owner with a spinal cord injury, I was invited to sponsor it by buying a table.

Being around other spinal cord injured people who were out there living life, being married, starting businesses, and otherwise being happy and gainfully employed invigorated me. I was not an anomaly that couldn't be replicated. It was my confirmation that a good life in with a spinal cord injury was there for those who wanted one.

I started to feel like as far as life was concerned, even with one kidney, I had finally arrived. I tried most of my life to make something of myself. All I ever wanted was for Lynn to be able to enjoy it with me. Now here I was, being the kind of business man I always hoped I'd be… without her.

But life goes on, as it always does. My family was around me, driving me nuts and keeping me sane at the same time. The business and Florida trips kept my mind occupied enough to not think about my cancer coming back until I had to do another ultrasound. I was always worked up as the dates drew near and so relieved when I got the all clear.

After a year, I was making enough money to consider a condo for myself in in Florida. The only place I wanted to be was my beloved Cocoa Beach. I started looking condos online in my spare time. It would have to be accessible for me and on the water. I flew down with Jimmy again once I had enough condos to see while I was there. It would only be a short trip so I had to line them up at the same time. The second condo was the one I fell in love with. It was a spacious two-bedroom, two-bath with a balcony on the second third floor. It had an outdoor elevator so I would have no trouble getting to my condo. I now had a place I could call home when I was at my beloved Cocoa Beach. I went out and bought all new furniture for my condo. My sister helped me decorate it and make it beachy and homey. We picked a calm color pallet of sea foam greens and beiges. I relaxed as soon as I saw it all together. Relaxing was something I was not accustomed to. I finally had a place and an excuse to do that. The hustle of life on the streets and scrapping to earn a living any way I could was stressful and wearying. Having a respite from the madness was what I needed.

I thought of Lynn and my dad. They both would have loved my condo. I sorrowed that neither one of them could enjoy what I had now. I could picture my dad walking around the condo complex and chatting it up with everyone he walked by. He was like that. He would have been up for hanging by the pool and trading stories with the other pool people. No one at my condo complex would ever know the joys of knowing Sal Paladino.

Life was good but I was looking for more. It's great to celebrate the wins in life but it isn't as much fun without someone to share it with. I started thinking of what it would be like to find someone to share it with for real this time. Was I ready to meet someone special?

I guess you are never really sure you are ready until you meet her. I wanted to realize the possibilities, rather than try and hang out with the local ladies in my area. I had already had it with meeting women in the little clubs where I used to go hear live music. I didn't want to date anyone's sister or friend. I did what any modern guy does. I put a profile on a few dating sites to see what meeting someone online would be all about.

Having to decide what to say about myself was hard. How do you sell yourself to someone who is looking? I supposed guys in chairs can handle broaching the subject a variety of ways. I thought it was best to be upfront about it. That way I'd weed out the ones who were not into it and I didn't have to wait to break it to anyone who might be uncomfortable with it. The chair isn't for everyone. I knew that going in. Once I got over what to say about myself and found some pictures I liked, I made my profiles go live. Who knew what would happen next. Was I supposed to wait for a reply?

Getting my profiles online made me interested in looking for prospects. I searched the sites to see who was on there. I looked at picture and read what they had to say about themselves. It was a little weird to consider women who were up there on the Internet for anyone who might be interested, but I was there. I quickly got over the uneasiness of Internet dating and started emailing some prospects for a conversation.

I never expected how entertaining meeting women online would be. Some of the craziest women are online looking to meet men for all kinds of reasons. Some of the women I started emailing were funny but not for me, others were full-on crazy. I never knew what emailed reply was going to come into my email box. I started to wonder if there was a normal lady out there looking to meet a handsome guy, such as myself.

I wondered if there was a woman out there was younger than me, maybe with a kid? I never had an opportunity to be a dad. I thought about what that would be like. Would I be open to a woman with a kid? I was older. I liked the life I had. I went to Florida whenever I wanted to. I could come and go as I pleased. Having a woman in my life, especially one with a child, would mean I couldn't do what I wanted to whenever I wanted to anymore. Was I ready for that?

I continued to answer replies and search online for the woman I would call mine. The weeks wore on and I started to wonder if it was possible. I had to admit, the conversations I had with the women I met online was a nice antidote to the loneliness that was settling in now that the weather had gone cold. The replies were like a warm blanket on a chilly night. It was fun to chat and get to know people, even if I wasn't really finding someone I wanted to get to know outside of the Internet. If nothing else, it was a great distraction from life and stress.

Soon it would be Christmas. Holidays always reminded me of who was not coming to Christmas Eve dinner at my sister Lisa's house. We always had dinner there, but the departed family members would not be with us. It is hard to remember Christmas Eves past and not sadden over who won't be there ever again. Another Christmas as a single man. I remembered what it was like to have Christmases with Lynn. I relived the fun surprises I'd have for her, the holiday decorating. It would be nice to share in the joys of the holidays with someone again.

Chapter 14 - The Sun Will Come Out Tomorrow

As was my usual thing to do on Saturday and Sunday mornings, I scrolled through the dating sites, looking at pictures and reading profiles. I came across a profile picture of a smiling woman with a beautiful face. I liked what I saw, so I scanned through her profile, looking for any glaring things that would steer me clear of connecting with her. I couldn't find anything glaringly wrong, so I emailed her. "Beautiful" was all I said.

Later on that day she emailed me back, "What is beautiful?" It was nice to get a simple reply. I told her, of course, that it was she that was I remarking about. She replied right away. The start of the conversation began.

We emailed off and on over the course of the next few days. We got through all the preliminary questions that two people who don't know each other have before they feel comfortable. One of the questions I had for her rocked me back a little. I asked her how old she was. She was 14 years younger than me! How did I miss this? *Did she know how old I was? Would a woman that much younger really be interested in me? Still, I liked talking to her so I kept emailing.* It was flattering to think that a beautiful younger woman would be interested in me. Was she?

She had questions for me, too. She was looking for a Christian guy. I happened to be one, but I wasn't necessarily advertising that. She asked me what my favorite bible verse was and she told me not to say, "John 3:16." I gave her the one I remembered most often, Isaiah 41:10 NIV:

"So do not fear, for I am with you; do not be dismayed, for I am your God. I will strengthen you and help you; I will uphold you with my righteous right hand."

She was satisfied with that statement, but asked me why it was my favorite. I didn't know I'd be pressed any further so I took a minute to think about what I would say. Apparently, she was looking for an answer to prove I was who I said I was in the religious department. I replied with the best reason I could think of. I thought it was valid. "Because God as always been with me." The conversation continued on that day so I knew I must have passed the test.

She texted me, a lot. It was hard to keep up with the replies. I was working during the day and my hands aren't that good to keep tying on a tiny phone keyboard. When I got frustrated enough, I told her she could always call me instead of text. I'd prefer to hear her voice anyway and plus I didn't have to work so hard at keeping up with the text volleys.

We started talking on the phone every night after her daughter went to bed. She would work out and then call me after she was done. I liked that she wanted to stay in shape. Most of the women my age where over the whole dieting and working out thing. *Would a woman who goes to the gym all the time want to hang out with a guy in a chair?*

Not matter how many times I tried to tally up the pluses in this budding relationship, the one minus always came back to me. She was too young and there was no way she was going to care about hanging out with me long term. But I liked talking to her. I decided it would be okay to flatter myself and let this thing continue. You know, see where it goes. I didn't have high hopes for it, though.

We went on about our nightly calls and daily texting for a couple of weeks. Maybe it went on too long. It took me three weeks to ask her for a date! She confessed on that phone call that if I didn't ask her out that week that she was going to assume I wasn't that interested. Not interested? I would have thought she was the one not interested, not me! We agreed to have her come to Connecticut to have dinner with me. She said she had a friend that could babysit that lived near me. The date was set. Exactly one week from that night, we'd be having dinner.

The more I thought about our impending first date, the more I got anxious. I had to wait a whole week and a lot can happen in that timeframe. Maybe she'd change her mind? Maybe I'd change my mind? I could be dead by next week.

On our call that following Sunday, I could hardly stand to contain myself with the anxiety when I blurted out, "I don't want to wait until next week, I want to come up and have lunch with you tomorrow." I waited for what felt like an eternity for an answer. Her reply?

"You'd drive all the way up here just to have lunch with me?"

I paused to take in what she just said. "Of course I would!"

The tricky part of my lunch date would be getting to Massachusetts and home in one piece. What she didn't know and what I don't really tell a whole lot of people is that I don't like driving on the highway. Me and anxiety have always been close companions and while I'd just assume he go find someone else to hang out with, he is always with me. Anxiety is always down to ride shotgun in the seat next to me. How was I going to get to Massachusetts without having a third wheel along for the ride? I couldn't meet her for the first time with someone with me so I wouldn't be scared driving. How was I going to handle this?

The first thing I did was call my friend Bo. He has known me since the THE EARLS days. We are in the regular habit of exchanging favors, so I called one in. I told him what my plans were for the next day and told him to clear his calendar. He'd be driving me to meet this woman for the first time. He thought I was nuts, but agreed to do it anyway. My plans were in place. Bo would drive me up to meet her for lunch and he'd go walk around the shopping center where the restaurant was so it didn't look like I had to have someone with me. I told him I'd give him a couple bucks for his troubles. That made him feel better about having to hang around a shopping center by himself while I had a nice lunch with a pretty lady.

I was jumping out of my skin for the rest of the day. *What was it going to be like? What would she think of me? Will she be just as good-looking in person as the picture I was enamored with?* There were so many questions and they would all be answered tomorrow. Maybe that is what I was so anxious about?

The drive from CT to Massachusetts seemed so long. I didn't remember it taking so long to get up there. I talked to Bo to get my mind off waiting to meet her. Finally, we made it up to some upscale shopping center in a town I'd never heard of in Massachusetts. I handed Bo some money to get lunch and told him to get lost until I texted him. I hopped into the driver's seat to make it look like I drove there. Once I got comfortable, I texted her to make sure she was there. She was. She was waiting for me in her car. I asked her to come up to my van. I told her I needed her to come out to me. She asked if I needed help. I didn't I just didn't want our first meeting to be in the middle of a busy restaurant. Talk about awkward! I watched out the windshield and scanned for her face. She came into view. She was prettier than I hoped. She was smiling and waving and walking toward me. I breathed out in relief.

She opened the passenger side door and I told her to get in. She looked a little puzzled but hopped into the van. I snapped my gum with nervousness as I said hello. We made the usual pleasantries about how my drive was and stuff. We drove around the block of the outdoor shopping center so I could find a handicapped spot. Once I parked I asked if I could kiss her. She looked surprised, but leaned in. Her kiss was gentle but purposeful. She felt like she wanted to kiss me. I was in heaven.

I slid out of the driver's seat of my van and into my chair. It felt effortless from the rush of kissing someone new. I wish they could make something that makes you feel that all the time. The first kiss is always the best one. You never get a second with the same woman.

We went into a trendy seafood restaurant on the corner of the shopping plaza. It smelled of seafood and spices and was humming loudly from all the commotion of shoppers and office people having lunch. Conversations and laughter spilled over from tables and booths. I hoped we could have a conversation in all this revelry. I guess good seafood lunches make people jovial. I wanted to steep in the joy that was her time more than I was interested in celebrating a good lunch.

We were seated at a spacious table near the bar. I didn't want distance between our chairs. I wanted to sit as close as possible to her. I wanted to feel the energy I felt when I kissed her some more. Food was irrelevant, but she said she was hungry, so I had to decide on what to eat. I was nervous, so I just had Manhattan clam chowder. It is my favorite, but there are not a lot of restaurants that have it. I was happy to see it on the menu. She got her favorite meal there. It was a dish with shrimp and rice with broccoli. It didn't look that interesting, but she said had to have it whenever she ate there. I would have rather had fish and chips but wasn't sure about the nervousness and the grease impacting my digestive system. People in chairs have to be mindful of all the possibilities. I struggled to think of how to begin the conversation so I took a lot of time to pretend I was pouring over the menu. She started. As it turns out, she is a great conversationalist so I didn't have to worry about what to say next. We mostly asked the usual questions about life and work and things we do when we are social. It was good to see her face when we were talking. All I had to go by before was how her voice sounded over the phone. I had enjoyed the fact that her voice was not annoying or high pitched. She didn't mumble or talk too loud. I has relieved to see that she was even prettier in person than she was in her picture. I settled in to listen to her talk and study her face. I knew right then and there that I wanted her to stay by my side from here on out.

Of course I didn't tell her that. I had to be the cool guy. You know, take it easy. I didn't want to scare her off either. Besides, it still occurred to me a lot that she was so much younger than me. I tried to brush those feelings off and just enjoy her company. She interrupted our conversation to say she had to visit the ladies' room. This would be my opportunity to catch her walking away. I saw the fullness of her frame as she walked away from me. Perfectly shapely in every way.

When she came back to the table our lunches arrived immediately. I was happy to focus on something else besides keeping up with the conversation. Lunch can do that. We set our minds and utensils on the task at hand. The chowder was almost as good as the company. I sat and ate, drinking her in, trying not to feel bad out my friend Bo out walking around an outdoor shopping plaza. It was a cold afternoon and I saw that it had started to rain when I glanced out the window to see if I could see him out there. Here I am having a great lunch with a beautiful lady while Bo freezes half to death so I can do this. I wanted to buy him something to eat, but didn't want to let on that I brought company so I decided not to.

We ate and shared a dessert. I was all I could do to make the lunch date last longer. She had coffee so I knew she'd be content to stay at least until it was gone. I pondered what it would be like to have her around and as I watched her face as she talked to me. She smiled a lot. I could get used to that.

Once I paid the bill, I asked her if she could come out the van with me. She watched me get in and help myself out of my chair and into the driver's seat again. I didn't want her to go home yet, so I asked her to get in. She did without asking why and we drove around the plaza again. I was looking for Bo. She thought we were just driving around. I had to let him know I was ready, so I texted him before we backed out of the space. Once I located him and told him I was ready, I had to see her off to her car. I was sad to leave her but happy that we still had our date planned for that coming Saturday. It was rather gentlemanly of me to come up to see her first, even if I hadn't exactly planned it that way. I sent her off with a long kiss and a promise to count the days until Saturday. She smiled at me for a moment and got out of the car. She asked me to call her when I got home. I like that she cared about me like that.

I pulled up next to a wet and freezing Bo. I motioned for him to get in. He looked reluctant to see me. I supposed I earned that leaving him outside like that for so long. He climbed in the van and asked, "So, how was it?"

I couldn't contain myself. I felt the words rush up before I could stuff them back down. "She's out of my league!" I couldn't help it. This girl was gonna hang out with me? I was panicked because I really liked her but I didn't want to put myself out there if she wasn't going to stick around. But I was so glad I got to spend lunch with her. I didn't want to leave. I wished I could have put her in my pocket and taken her home with me. She lived all the way up near Boston, and she had a kid. How was this going to work? The negative thoughts rushed around while Bo asked questions and I answered. I got so wrapped up in talking about our date with Bo that I didn't realize I got on the wrong highway. It wasn't until nearly an hour in the wrong direction before I realized I was heading for Rhode Island, not Connecticut!

Once I got over the shock realizing I was nowhere near home about an hour into my drive, I had to figure out how to get back on track. I knew how to get there but there was no easy course correction from Rhode Island to New Britain. I'd just have to ride it out. It would take me another two hours to get home. Once I was well past my expected time of arrival at home, Brittany started texting me to see if I was okay. I couldn't answer her as I was nervous from driving and having to get back in the right direction. As the time went by, the calls and texts became more frequent and urgent. She was worried that something happened. I pained with every new message. I wanted to tell her everything was fine, it was just that I made wrong turn, but I couldn't. It was night time now and I hate driving at night. I had to keep both hands on the wheel, undistracted by the new shiny thing I wanted to call mine. As soon as I dropped Bo off, I sent the relief to her that she needed. "I'm fine. Just got home. Will call later."

When I phoned her for our nightly call, she picked it up on half a ring. "What happened?"

I had to explain that I had gotten lost and how much time it took me to get back to CT. I left out the reason for getting lost was talking about her. She was just relieved that I was okay.

"I would feel so bad if something happened to you on the way home. Your family would have hated me!"

We had a good laugh about it during our short conversation. I was exhausted from the getting lost ordeal, plus the ride up and back to Boston in one day (with a stop in RI in between). I told her I wanted to lay down for the night. She understood. I said my goodnights and went to be dreaming of the next time I would see her in person.

Saturday was here before I knew it. It was going to be Brittany's birthday the next week but I had already booked my trip to my condo in Florida so I had to think fast. I wanted to make a big impression. This was our official first date and now that I knew I wanted her to stick around, I had to up my efforts. I sent my niece Chelsea off to the mall to buy her a small birthday gift. Something nice but not too nice. I wanted to come off as thoughtful, not desperate.

I planned a nice dinner at my favorite local Italian place. I knew the owner well so we'd be given some extra special care. I had a friend who owned a flower shop so I had Scott send a dozen red roses to the restaurant for the table that night. I wanted everything to be perfect. I thought I thought of everything. The one thing I didn't plan on is for it to turn out to be the coldest night of the year. The temperature on Saturday night plummeted to under 10 degrees. I didn't want have to do this, but between the ice and the cold, I couldn't be outside in frigid weather like that. I asked if she'd mind if we had dinner at my house instead. Thankfully, she agreed. She would have to go to her friend Jenn's house with her daughter Carli and get her settled, and then she'd come on over.

I made sure my personal care attendant picked out the best outfit for me. I wanted to be looking sharp. Once she left, it was just me until she arrived. The waiting was agony. I rolled around and around my apartment, looking for anything out of place. The minutes went by like hours. Finally, there was a knock at the door. It was here. She was here.

It is always awkward the first few minutes of someone coming over to your house for the first time. I nervously showed her around my apartment. I kept the lights dimmed to set a romantic mood, and had candles lit for extra effect. I wanted her to feel comfortable and relaxed. She smiled and acknowledged the effort I made. I had a bottle of wine opened for her. I figured maybe she'd like a glass to take the edge off. Plus, wine goes great with Italian fare. I knew I'd feel better if I could see that she was relaxed. Within minutes the delivery man arrived with our food. I sent by brother to the restaurant while I was waiting to fetch the flowers. She was delighted to see them come through the door. With food here, we now had something to focus on.

I asked her what she wanted to have for dinner before she came. She ordered chicken cacciatore, commenting that it was her favorite. I liked learning new things about her. I ordered chicken parmesan. It wasn't the healthiest thing to have but it made me happy. We ate and talked about the ride down for her. It is a long drive and it involved having to get her eight-year-old daughter acquainted with a new place before she could come over. The ride from her friend's house to here was another 45 minutes. She made quite an effort to come see me. I appreciated that. But I did get hopelessly lost getting home from seeing her on Monday, so I supposed we were even.

The wine flowed even after dinner. That night, nothing mattered but the two of us. I presented her with her birthday gifts after we had time to digest. She was surprised that I considered getting her a birthday gift so soon in our relationship. I was comforted by her delight in what she received. She sparkled as she thanked me for them. Roses and birthday gifts. She poured over my efforts to please her. She commented that she'd never had nice a nice first date in her whole life. That's when I knew I did good. We sat in my living room and talked about life and past loves. The glow of the candles danced on her face and I studied her as she spoke. The furrow of her brow, the light of her smile, she captivated me. I wanted to kiss her. I thought of how I could do it without seeming like I was trying to take advantage. I took her hand while she was talking and when she paused, I pulled her in. To kiss her made the frigid night disappear and I could feel the ice crystals in my heart melting for her.

Chapter 15 - Can Lightning Strike Twice?

I went to my condo in Florida the day after my first official date with Brittany with a fire in my heart and a joy in my soul that had not been there in years. I spent my brief, early morning flight reliving the details of the night before. She was smart and she was beautiful. And she was so much younger than me. I felt my mind tracing her every curve of her face as I thought out our conversations. Was she really going to hang out with a guy like me? I've had no problem finding dates, don't get me wrong, but not like her.

I asked her to text me when she got home the next day. I was happy to see that she arrived safely and made sure she let me know. I couldn't help but wish she was there with me. I wanted to continue what we started. The welcoming sun I always felt when I came to Florida was now somehow overshadowed by her absence. Was I getting attached too soon?

I tried reasoning with myself that I shouldn't get too involved. That she'd come to her senses soon and realize that a relationship with this kind of age difference wasn't for her. However, when I texted her, she responded right away. It didn't help that she was so attentive to me. Some of my friends and family members thought I was crazy when I told them that she had a daughter and a 14-year age difference. I wanted to believe them, but she drew me in.

I had the love of my life in my life for 28 years. Could I love another woman like that again? I wanted to believe that I could. I just didn't know if it would happen. I liked the idea of finding out if something real was starting with Brittany, though. I decided to see where his would go. Even if most people I knew told me that I would live to regret it.

I became interested in when we could see each other again and how that would practically work. We agreed that we would alternate visits between Connecticut and Boston, with the visitor staying in a hotel. That was agreeable to her, although it presented a bit of a challenge for me. I can't really drive on the highway. How was I going to make this work without telling her? I started lining up drivers on the weekends I knew I'd have to go to Boston. It wasn't that easy though. I also had to get my drivers to agree to stay in a hotel overnight by themselves while I was with her. When I got people to commit to taking me, I relaxed a little. Then the weekend came for me to visit. She was excited to have me come up and see her house and where she lived. I was hoping the driver arrangements would work out while pretending that I was excited too and looking forward to seeing her. I was, of course, looking forward to being with her. I just was concerned about it not working out and what I would have to say to her if it didn't. But the weekend came and all was well. My friend Bo drove me up to Boston again and I got him settled in his own hotel with enough money to order food and pretended that he didn't exist for a night. We had dinner at the hotel that I was staying at. It was a contemporary Marriott with dark, hip bar. It was the perfect place for hanging out with a beautiful woman.

Her smile when she saw me captivated me. She smiled with her whole face as she walked toward me. I relaxed when I embraced her and kissed her 'hello.' I felt good when I was around her. She was attentive to me, I liked that. I mattered to her. We settled into the restaurant for dinner. The lights were low and the room was dark brown with deep red accents. The kind of vibe you get from upscale steakhouses. We were presented with our menus and chatted as we poured over the options. She ordered wine right away. A nice red this time. Note to self: She likes wine.

I wish I liked wine but my taste for it was soured a long time ago when I was a teen and we'd pass around the jugs of Martini and Rossi and I'd drink it until I stumbled around and vomited. I've had no interest in it ever since. Even though I am not a drinker, I found myself ordering a Heineken to join her. Being with her made me feel celebratory.

The whole night felt like a beautiful song. I didn't want it to end, but we had both agreed we'd attend her church the next day, so staying up all night was not an option. I liked that she had a faith in God. It made me feel good about her character. I had just never dated a girl who loved God as much as she did. She was a Bible teacher. I didn't really know much about the Bible, other than what I had heard from my own church. I wondered if I could keep up with her when it came to stuff like that. I was curious to see what kind of church she went to. I figured it would tell me a lot about her. Like if she was a normal Jesus lover or if she was a total religious nut job or something. You can find out a lot about a person by going to their church.

Once I attended the first service with her, I could put my mind to rest that she wasn't crazy. I really enjoyed her church, actually. It was different than mine, but I really love the pastor and the environment in general. It was an old warehouse converted into a church. There was a fun element to it all, along with a strong message I could get into.

We had lunch right after and that's when I found myself getting anxious. Bo had been up a while by now and was interested in finding out when we were heading home. It was a two-hour drive and he had things to do back in CT. While we had lunch she was completely clueless that I was going back and forth with Bo over when we were leaving. I had to come up with a good enough excuse as to why I had to wrap things up right after lunch. I found the best one I could: football. Since she was a football fan herself, she easily bought into the need to jet out of there over getting home in time to watch the 4-o'clock game. I was relieved that my reason to depart was met without questions and we decided to get lunch over with sooner, rather than later so Bo wouldn't be upset with me for making him wait alone in some hotel room for an undetermined amount of time.

When I met up with Bo, he had all kinds of questions. He was curious to know if I still felt the same way about her now that I spent the weekend hanging out with her. I didn't want to give away too much, but I had a great time. I could see myself spending a lot of time with her. Suddenly the age difference wasn't a big worry for me anymore. I recounted the details to him that I wanted to share while we drove and then I changed the subject to football and guy stuff.

When I left, she and I agreed she'd come visit me. That was a relief. All I had to do was get her a hotel room so she'd have somewhere to stay. *Was the distance going to be a problem for us over the long haul?* I started to ponder that question more seriously. Now that I was getting comfortable with the age difference, my mind shifted to the practicality that a guy like me would be able to go back and forth to Boston every other weekend. I couldn't drive myself so I'd have to line up people to help me make the trip, all without letting on to her that I wasn't the one making the trek. Bo would be my driver on the weekends I had go up to Boston, along with my friend Gerald, my nephew Paulie, and sister, Lisa. No one was particularly excited about the prospect, but they were willing to help, even if it was begrudgingly.

With my drivers lined up for the near future, it was smoother sailing. I could relax in knowing logistics were not as much of an issue. Now that driving was out other way, I found a new thing to focus on: her daughter.

Lynn and I didn't have kids. We took our nieces and nephews for a sleepover every once in a while, but that is different than raising kids. That I didn't know anything about. What would it be like to have a kid around all the time, a girl no less? Would she like me? Would I like her? Having a kid involved in your relationship puts a whole new twist on things. I thought about what would happen if her daughter came between us. It happens to couples all the time. Did I want a kid to be in the mix of my life? I always wanted a family of my own, though. I found myself daydreaming about the possibilities of being a dad. It was worth the risk.

After a few more weekends of dates, we both felt comfortable with the way things were going. Every weekend together was a good one. I found myself reviewing last weekend in my mind and daydreaming about what the next one would be like. We talked on the phone every night and texted all day long. She was a welcomed distraction to my work, but my employees were getting short on patience with me. I couldn't focus. Being a relationship with a beautiful, smart woman after all this time gave me new life. There were exciting adventures to look forward to with someone again.

One night while we were on the phone she brought up the subject of meeting her daughter, Carli. This was a big step. It also let me know that as far as she was concerned, this was serious enough to involve her daughter. She asked me what I thought. I waded into this conversation carefully. Of course I wanted to meet her, but was it a little soon? I was also anxious to get the awkwardness of the first meeting with her out of the way. I agreed that the next time she came down to CT we'd have a meetup, the three of us.

The weekend came to meet her and I found myself being apprehensive. Everything going forward hinged on this weekend going well. Whatever happened couldn't be undone. There was no going back now.

We were meeting for dinner the hotel I had arranged for them to stay at. We would meet in the lobby and eat at the hotel. It would just be easier. That way we wouldn't have to jump in and out of cars. For me, if this meeting went south, I could just bag out of there and be home in ten minutes. I didn't know what to expect. I wanted to like her. I wanted her to like me. I knew this going well would make Brittany happy. We could both relax into the next stage of this relationship once this speed bump was behind us. I was a on edge, but made myself believe it would all be fine. Besides, I didn't have much of a choice.

I wheeled around the lobby of the hotel, pacing as I waited for them to walk in. Finally, the doors parted and in they strolled. Much to my relief, as soon as Carli was introduced to me, she threw her eight-year-old little arms around my neck and hugged me. Her greeting melted any fears I had that this would go astray. The hug solidified my faith in this relationship. This could be something good for me. Was the family I dreamed of within my grasp?

Dinner went as planned. We had a great night of hanging out with Carli so I could get to know her. She was very interested in me and chattering on about herself. Her animated demeanor was entertaining and dizzying at the same time. I had forgotten how eight-year-old little girls are. Everything was exciting to her.

I made my way home when it started getting near to Carli's bedtime. We agreed to go to church the next morning and have lunch afterwards. I was so happy with everything that I didn't even mind driving myself home in the dark.

It's always weird to introduce someone to your church. You never know what their experiences with churches are or how they will relate to it. I didn't have kids so I had no idea what going to my church would be like for Carli or if they would have a program for her. We wandered in, all in our Sunday best. Luckily, there was something for kids on Sundays at my church. That was a relief.

After church we went to eat at one of my favorite restaurants, Joey Garlic's. Carli was a picky eater so choosing a restaurant with something she'd eat was at the forefront of her mother's mind. Pasta, being one of Carli's favorite choices, was a guarantee at Joey Garlic's. The restaurant was loud and distracting. We tried to talk while we ate, but the people and servers crowding around us and the swarm of noise the swirled above our heads made it hard to concentrate on spending time together. After we ate, we decided maybe we could wheel around the mall and hang out. Besides, there isn't much to do in the wintertime for a guy in a chair anyway. Roaming the mall was our best hope to keep a child entertained and us spending more time together. We wandered the halls, holding hands and trying to pay attention to Carli darting around and pointing out all the things she thought were interesting. It seems everything is interesting at the mall to a girl that age.

Alas, soon enough it was time for them to venture home when we ran out of mall and the early afternoon bled into the early evening. It was the weekend I hoped it would be. Brittany was beaming from ear to ear so I knew we did a good job with introductions. What the future held for us I do not know, but I did know it would include a child and it seemed the child was okay with that.

We continued to do things as a threesome on most weekends. Sometimes that got in the way of my wanting to spend time with her. But I understood. There were some weekends when she could leave Carli with her mother, those were the weekends we grew closer together as a couple. Things really solidified for me when I invited Brittany and Carli to Florida with me for the first time. I knew this would make or break us. We had a great time. I could see my future with her. That made me make plans that looked like she would be in it.

I like to flip houses to make extra money so when a house went up for sale in one of the nicest neighborhoods nearby, I decided to go look at it. I thought it would be a good way to make a quick buck but when I took pictures of it and showed them to Brittany, her reply was "No matter what you do to that house it will still be ugly." Not that she was the reason I turned the house down but I knew she was right. It was just not an attractive house on the outside.

As I made my way home, I noticed another house for sale. It was a beautiful ranch that sat at the back of a large plot of land with a fish pond greeting you at the beginning of the winding driveway. My curiosity was piqued and I turned in to have a better look. The house sat on the top of a cliff of rock that overlooked a valley with a golf course at the bottom. This house sat overlooking the tee box to the fifth hole. I had never seen such a spectacular view from anyone's house before in my life. It had a large deck that spanned the entire back of the house, perfect for entertaining and view gazing.

I wheeled back to my van to call my real estate agent and tell her about the house. "I want to see what this house looks like on the inside," I told her. The next thing I knew she was in the driveway and calling for the code to get the key. The front of the house was perfectly landscaped. Flowers and shrubs all neatly manicured and purposefully placed for maximum wow effect. Once we were in, I had a look around. The front door introduced a large entryway to an open concept house. The back of the house was lined with French doors that beckoned the sunlight in. The hallways were wide and the rooms spacious. I had an easy time maneuvering every room with the chair, even the bathrooms which is almost always the challenge in any house.

My mouth gaped as I took it all in. I grew up on the other side of town where one could only dream of living on the West End. Back then, houses like this only belonged to doctors, lawyers, and executives from the hardware factories in town. A kid like me who grew up blue collar never imagined we'd ever have the opportunity to move into a house like this. When I could take the suspense no longer, I asked how much. It was more than I had ever paid for a house, but it was well within my reach. The real estate agent asked if I wanted to put in an offer in. Did I?

I called Brittany back to tell her about the house. She was excitedly asking me to send pictures of what I saw, but what I had could not really do it justice. I told her I'd take her to see it if it was still for sale when she came that weekend. My mind ran away with me when I got home. Should I buy this house? Living with my family upstairs from me in the third family was great in some respects but they also drove me crazy. I knew that Brittany, Carli, and I would be cramped in my two-bedroom apartment. Could we have a life in this house just a couple miles down the street?

Before I could talk myself out of it, I was showing Brittany and my sisters the house. I put an offer in to secure the house while I finished up deciding. The house was mine in a matter of weeks. Now that I had the proper house for a family, I had to make my relationship with Brittany official. I set out to find the perfect ring and proposal plan for the second girl of my dreams.

I planned to propose in Miami at a beautiful hotel with lots of pomp and circumstance but three weeks before our trip I came down with the flu. It hit me so hard I could barely get out of bed for a week. Even after three weeks, I was still weak and tired easily. That put a heavy lid of my creativity for working out the perfect proposal scenario. I just didn't have the energy for it. I popped the question at dinner I had planned at the hotel. I did manage to work out with the restaurant manager when I wanted to propose during dinner. Everything went as planned. She said yes and our plans to be a family were a real thing now.

Our wedding was sweet and small. Just family and a handful of friends. After much deliberation over where and when to have it, we settled on February at our house. The day came together spectacularly. In a matter of hours, our house was transformed from a home to an intimate wedding venue with flowers everywhere. It was a stunning and surprising sight for us all. Our "I Dos" were celebrated with dinner and cupcakes from our favorite gourmet cupcake place. We honeymooned in Florida, of course. My new life with my new wife and stepdaughter in my beautiful house that I never dreamed I'd ever own was reality.

Chapter 16 - Letting Go of a Dear Old Friend

I had been at this medical supply business thing for ten years now. It had fallen into a rhythm and we saw growth in the company every year. My little business became a multi-million-dollar company. I had not just one, but a half a dozen people working for me. I had my own office and people called me "Boss." I was the person I always wanted to be. I was just a little sad that Lynn never got to see what I'd built. It was always my hope that the life I had built now would have been the one I could give her. But that was not mean to be.

The business had become something more than I wanted to deal with. With so many customers, there were plenty of headaches that came with it. Life was more manageable for New Britain Medical Supplies when I only had to deal with Medicare and Medicaid. Now I had major insurance contracts and a company my size has a lot of regulations to consider. Big insurance companies get to tell you how you do business with them. Every contract had its own hoops to jump through. I was tired of always having to consider them. I just wanted to come in and talk to my customers. I didn't want to have to shovel my way through bureaucracy and red tape what felt like every day.

When you have a lot of employees, you also have to deal with interpersonal issues in the office. You'll have to forgive my saying this, but having an office full of women has an added stress when it comes to dealing with infighting. There always seemed to be some squabble between employees that I had to deal with. Each one would occupy my office to pour words of frustration over a coworker into my ears. I wanted to escape it. I am a good businessman, but I am not a good human resources manager. I just wanted everyone to get along and leave me out of it.

Every time I went to Florida to go visit what went from a small condo with just me and a friend to a house with a boat on the water with a wife and stepdaughter, I just wished I could stay there indefinitely. I would go for a week every month, return and then wile away the hours until I could go again. It is not that I didn't like having a family at home and a thriving business to deal with. It was that the stress of all of these great things in my life were mounting up and I wanted to relieve the pressure somehow. Some days I felt like a pressure valve that was ready to blow. I didn't like feeling like I was moments away from exploding on someone.

I had entertained offers to buy my business before. Some of them were ridiculous. I was offered $400,000 for my company when it was small, but after attorneys and taxes I would hardly be wheeling away with anything to show for it. Plus, I felt like the time and money I spent getting the business to where it was well worth more than I was being offered. What I did was worth something, even if the person writing a check for it didn't think so. I bid them farewell and no hard feelings, but I wanted more than they thought it was worth.

Here and there companies much larger than mine would phone me to say they'd be interested in talking about a deal to acquire us. By the time serious inquiries started coming in, we were in the office space and I had a nice list of insurance contracts that larger companies would be interested in buying us for. Insurance companies were being choosy about who was in network to work with their members. Basically, if you didn't have a contract with them by now, you were not getting one. The fact that I had amassed the list I had made me attractive to them. I had Connecticut Medicaid also, which is like the holy grail of insurance contracts. That was the subject that always came up in meetings to acquire us. They wanted to know what they could expect to make off of Medicaid from my contract. Medicaid billing is easy money and they wanted in. I just wasn't going to give it away to the lowest bidder.

I loved my customers. A lot of them I got to know personally. Whenever they had a problem, they had my cell number to call me and straighten it out. I didn't want the "be one of the family" culture I had created to disappear as soon as I cashed the check. I wanted to be sure whoever acquired New Britain Medical had a good reputation. That stance helped me show plenty of subpar medical supply companies the door before they even sipped their first cup of coffee in my conference room. New Britain Medical Supplies' reputation was something to consider. That's the way I built it and it is what gave us such a stunning competitive edge over our enormously sized competitors.

The more I considered interested companies, the more I thought about what retirement would look like. The freedom to do what I wanted to do was within my reach and well before most people would be able to retire. I relished the notion that I had built something from nothing that would provide for me to live comfortably in retirement. Most walking people can't even say that. I simply wanted whatever offer I accepted to make it worth my while. Nothing that had come across so far peaked my interest enough to seriously consider.

I dreamed of being able to spend as much time in Florida as I could, as soon as I could get out from under New Britain Medical Supplies. At the same time, I worried what that future would look like for my customers and my employees. It was an emotional tug of war that went on in my mind. Yes, I wanted no responsibilities and the freedom to fish and watch swaying palm trees whenever I wanted to. No, I didn't want to hear from customers and former employees that they were not happy.

The truth is, the business needed more than I could give it to grow more. We were pretty maxed out on resources as it was. Did I want to see it explode into the abyss of success? At times. I could have hired someone more qualified than me in business to run it if I wanted to go in that direction. I just didn't like the idea of handing the keys over completely to someone else and trust that they would do it the justice I did. No one is ever going to love your business like you do. I knew that.

In the middle of all of this, my beloved mother started to take a turn. She wasn't handling her medications well anymore. She was anxiety ridden and needed constant reassurance. She needed to be hospitalized a few times to deal with some issues she had been having that no one seemed to have a good handle on. It worried me that she wasn't getting better and no one was entirely sure what was wrong with her. The stress of the business and the worrying over my mother was wearing on me. I felt on edge. Losing her was not something I could even bring myself to think about. Not now. She still hadn't seen my house in Florida yet! I always wanted to bring her but she always told me, "Next time." I looked forward to the day when she could see it. Now, I worried that she never would. I wanted the doctors to hurry up and get her better so she could go. Just one time.

I was approached one day by email from a massive company in Europe. They were a global manufacturer of one brand of catheters and they were interested in making an offer to acquire us. Just like all the others, I welcomed them to have a conversation with me about it. I wasn't going to get my hopes up about anything spectacular in the way of offers. The ones I came across so far were too low for me to be interested. Nevertheless, it never hurts to have a conversation. Especially if that conversation comes with a lot of zeros on a check.

I talked to Brittany about it and my sisters. Should I entertain this? We had so much going on with Mom. Everyone thought it wouldn't be bad to at least hear them out. I had to keep it quiet, though. I didn't want my staff to get nervous about a sale before it was time to consider them. They sent over their nondisclosure agreements and I signed them. They were officially serious about considering a purchase.

I was a little surprised by all the information they wanted to pour over before they'd consider a figure. I had a lot of things to gather and calculate. They asked for figures I hadn't considered keeping track of. At one point it was so much information that I considered telling them to forget the whole thing. I worried they would just ask for all of this and walk away. This went on for a couple of months. With every email for more information, I sighed and wondered what I had gotten myself into. By now, I had my billing manager combing through records and making spreadsheets for everything they wanted. The work was dizzying. At the same time, I was surprised by how much New Britain Medical Supplies had accomplished. I knew I did well, but seeing it in print was another level of confirmation that I had built something worth being proud of. All with an 8th-grade education.

Finally, the calculations were in. They were ready to make an offer. I wanted to know but I was afraid to be disappointed. I speculated, got excited, and then convinced myself it would be something I couldn't go through with. When the email came with their offer, I didn't know if I could open it. Would this really be it? Is this the offer I was waiting for?

I open the email and got clammy as the attachment opened. I was pleasantly surprised by the large number I saw in on the screen. I could hardly contain my excitement when I called my wife to tell her what it was. Who would have thought that a simple guy like me in a chair since he was 16 would have the kind of retirement account that doctors and lawyers would envy?

I had to accept the offer to go forward. That was the hardest part. Did I want to agree to this? Could I get more if I just waited a little? The writing had been on the wall for a while now, though. My industry was changing. Large companies like this one were buying up small shops like me all over the country. The plan was to eliminate the middle man, and just go direct to consumer. I was another little guy in the way of world domination for these people. Even if I stayed around, there was no guarantee that I would not be edged out in a few years. I decided that being greedy wouldn't serve me well in the end. After much consideration, conversation, calculation, and lost sleep, I signed the offer. We were entertaining the biggest decision I ever made in my life.

It would be great to say that they just sent me a check and I wheeled off into the sunset to drink beer on my boat and go fishing but it doesn't work that way. The next phase of acquisition involved lots of lawyers and forensic accountants all looking to poke holes in my business to negotiate down with. They went over every last decimal point and word in the contracts. I was grateful to have been referred to one of the best acquisition firms in the country to help me. I didn't know anything about legal advice for something like this. We went back and forth on findings and contract stipulations for what felt like a decade. In the middle of this, my mother ended up in the hospital again.

My mother had been complaining that she didn't want to eat because her food wouldn't go down. We had no idea what she was talking about and she wasn't really saying much about it other than that she didn't want to eat because she couldn't swallow. But the last trip to the hospital gave her a diagnosis we hadn't heard before. My mother's throat wasn't closing over her windpipe to keep food and drink out of her lungs. She was aspirating whatever she ate or drank. That conversation from the doctors sent up reeling. What did that mean?

They said that they could not fix it with surgery. My poor mom, who had loved me from birth, was now going to suffer with this condition until she passed. I sorrowed over this revelation. I didn't want her to go through this. Her return home involved hospice. Within a couple of weeks, she passed. I didn't know I could be so heartbroken. What would I do without her?

Trying to close on an acquisition in the middle of losing your mother is one of the hardest things I could ever do. I doubt I have really even processed it all still.

On a sunny October day, with my beautiful wife by my side, I signed the final papers to sell my company. It was the best and the worst day of my life. New Britain Medical Supplies was the girl I never wanted to let go of, yet she was walking out the door with another because I told her it was time to say goodbye.

I stayed on for a few years to ease the transition with employees and customers, but it wasn't the same. They didn't want me to do too much and I struggled with where my place was there. I was like watching your ex-girlfriend kiss another guy. I spent the last year of the contract longing for my release. I wanted to let it all go, walk away and say it was over. I also wanted my final lumpsum payment they owed me for sticking around. The day came at long last. I said so long to her one last time, and New Britain Medical Supplies was married to someone else.

Life after the sale looked a lot different than I imagined. In some ways I struggled to find a new identity outside of New Britain Medical Supplies. In other ways, I was overwhelmed with choice as to what to do next. Eventually, I settled into a new routine, but I am not sure it will be as much of a thrill ride as building my company was. I get to spend a lot more time with the people I love, I know that. Was it all worth it? It sure was. Man, what a strange trip this has been, but I owe it all to God. I am the most unlikely comeback story, but here I am telling you about it. What kind of life can you make for yourself out of the ashes of bad decisions? That's up to you, and the one who made you.

CPSIA information can be obtained
at www.ICGtesting.com
Printed in the USA
BVHW012225090722
641764BV00003B/89